THINK OF A HOTDOG.

If the picture that comes to mind is a wiener in a bun with mustard, think again!

Here are just a few of the many ways you can use this popular and versatile taste tempter:

>   Spice up your next party with a hotdog appetizer

>   Take the chill out of winter with a hearty hotdog soup

>   Keep your cool in summer with a piquant hotdog salad

>   Make he-men happy with a hefty hotdog casserole

>   Cater to kids with a happy hotdog cookout

>   Stretch your budget with an economical hotdog main dish

And best of all, satisfy that gourmet cook who lives within *you* by whipping up an epicurean hotdog delight.

OTHER BOOKS BY THE SAME AUTHOR

THE NEW
HOTDOG
COOKBOOK

Mettja C. Roate

MB
A MACFADDEN-BARTELL BOOK

CONTENTS

THE NEW
HOTDOG
COOKBOOK

Chapter I

INTRODUCTION
TO THE HOT DOG

WIENERS, FRANKFURTERS, franks or hot dogs are the all-encompassing titles given to this most delicious and best-known sausage. Though no one in America needs an introduction to the hot dog, to many people it simply means a wiener in a long bun with mustard and relish oozing from its open side. That is one way to serve this delicious sausage. There are many other ways to use delicious, tasty wieners in cooking; this book will give them to you.

Seasoned ground meat held captive in a casing goes way back into ancient history. Who invented the wiener or hot dog as we know it today is open to claim and debate. One school of thought maintains that it was invented in the 1850's by an enterprising Austrian. He named his sausage "Wien" after Vienna, Austria. There is another school of thought which maintains that the hot dog was invented by an ambitious butcher in Frankfort on Main in Germany at about the same time. He called his tasty sausages "Frankfurters."

The fellow who put the long bun around the wiener came from St. Louis. His brother-in-law was selling hot wieners sans bun at the St. Louis Exposition in 1904. In order to facilitate eating these hot wieners, he furnished his customers with sanitary white cotton gloves. The customers were supposed to return the gloves for laundering so that they could be used over and over again. You know human nature and forgetfulness. The gloves walked.

The wiener salesman took up the problem with his brother-in-law who was a baker. No doubt one hot summer evening they were discussing the pitfalls of owning a business and free enterprise. The dilemma of the walking gloves was brought up, and the baker-brother-in-law came forth with the idea of a long bun to exactly fit that wiener. They tried it, and it worked. Soon after, beautifully-gowned ladies and cut-away-coated gentlemen were strolling arm in arm chomping away on America's new lunch on-the-go—the hot dog.

Where the wiener in a bun really made its big mark, of course, was at Coney Island in New York. The gentleman who put the hot dog into the everyday vocabulary of the U. S. A. was Mr. Nathan Handwerker. When he started his very first "Nathan's Famous Coney Island Hot Dog Stand," people were dubious of a sandwich that cost a mere five cents.

Legend has it that Mr. Handwerker hired a group of handsome, wholesome-looking young men, dressed them in starched white coats, put a stethoscope in each outside breast pocket with just enough of the instrument showing to identify the young man possibly as an intern or young doctor. The legend goes on to relate that all these young men had to do for their wages was to cheerfully munch Nathan's five-cent wiener sandwiches in front of his stand. Naturally, people noticed these young wiener-munching "doctors" and the rumor got around that if the doctors ate and liked the five-cent wiener sandwiches, they had to be good and be good for you.

The rest of the story reads like a success epic. Mr. Handwerker had his special mixture of good beef, spices and garlic. To this day, Nathan's wieners are some of the most delicious and best known in the world.

The wiener is just about 115 years old, and it continues to grow in popularity with each new generation. In the United States we consume 80 wieners yearly per person on the average. That comes to enough wieners to make about three round trips to the moon if they were laid end to end.

When buying hot dogs, always purchase those that have the name of a reputable meat packer on them. Off brands can be off flavor. There are many makers of wieners in the U. S. A. When you find a nationally known or regional brand that is to your complete liking, stay with it to avoid disappointment.

Each meat packer has his own secret formula for making his particular brand of wieners. Flavors vary from brand to brand, often due to the amount and kinds of spices used. They may also vary in the actual type of meat content. One packer may use all beef; another may use a mixture of beef and pork; still another may use portions of beef, pork and veal. However, all packers use only Government-inspected meats and all wieners are made under the most rigid conditions of their particular formula.

The fresh, lean meat that goes into wieners is carefully weighed; then it is finely ground. It is automatically measured after grinding so that each hot dog in your package is uniform. The finely ground, seasoned and measured meat is then put into casings or molds. Then the sausages are smoked for many hours over hardwood fires which often contain hickory wood and apple wood. It is through this slow, patient smoking that the wiener takes on its succulent flavor and wonderful appetizing color.

After smoking, the wieners are cooked again in either hot water or live steam. After this second thorough cooking, the wieners are rapidly chilled and then packaged. Immediately after this chilling and packaging, they are rushed to your local market so that you will always be able to purchase them at their flavor peak. Rest assured that when you buy that package of wieners in your market, you are buying thoroughly cooked meat without a fraction of an ounce of waste.

Hail to the Hot Dog! It is wonderful protein food, equally good for young and old. Wieners contain the same top protein and meat value as very lean steaks and roasts. To be sure you are getting this pure meat, always read the labels on the wieners you purchase. If there has been any filler such as corn meal, wheat or soybean flour used, the packer's label, according to Federal law, must state this fact.

If you have only eaten wieners in the usual bun, mustard and relish manner, try some of the wonderful recipes in this book. Wieners are made from only the purest ground lean meat. They are delicately seasoned and delicately smoked. Above all, wieners are always fully cooked before they reach your shopping cart making them a truly time-saving, economical, delicious source of protein and energy for your family.

Chapter II

HOT DOG HORS D'OEUVRES

Because of their ruddy, inviting color and delicate flavor, hot dogs make some of the most delicious hors d'oeuvres you'll ever have the pleasure of serving.

Since all hot dogs come to you already cooked, preparation time for hors d'oeuvres is cut down to a minimum. Your tray can take on the hues and tones of a painting by the simple addition of olives, parsley, cheese and pimientos.

If you want to tease and please appetites, use hot dogs in making your appetizers; you will rate an accolade of praise from your family and guests.

HOT DOG AND CUKE SPREAD

6 hot dogs
1 5-inch cucumber
¼ cup chili sauce
½ cup mayonnaise
12 slices enriched white bread, crusts removed

Chop the hot dogs until they are the consistency of coarse corn meal. Peel the cucumber, leaving on a bit of the green skin. Cut the cucumber in half lengthwise. Using a teaspoon, scrape away the seeds and center pulp, discard. Cut up the cucumber halves into ½-inch pieces and then chop until the consistency of coarse corn meal.

Combine the chopped hot dogs, chopped cucumber, chili sauce and mayonnaise. Mix well, then spread on six slices of the white bread; top each with another slice of bread. Cut into "finger" sandwiches. Arrange on a tray in layers with wax paper between the layers and place in the refrigerator at least 2 hours before serving. Makes 24 finger sandwiches.

HOT DOG SAUERKRAUT APPETIZERS

¼ cup butter
½ cup onion, finely chopped
1 clove garlic, finely chopped
2 tablespoons parsley, finely chopped
6 hot dogs, chopped to hamburger consistency
1 beef bouillon cube dissolved in ½ cup hot water
¼ cup all-purpose flour
1 #2 can sauerkraut
½ cup all-purpose flour (additional)
2 eggs, beaten until lemon yellow
¼ cup half-and-half cream
2 cups pretzel crumbs, made from crushed cocktail
   pretzel sticks
Vegetable oil for deep frying

Melt the butter in a suitable saucepan. Add the onion, garlic and minced parsley. Saute over low heat until the onion is tender and transparent. Stir in the chopped hot dogs. Mix ¼ cup flour and the bouillon water until it is smooth and free of lumps. Add to the hot dog mixture and stir until well blended.

Drain the sauerkraut; using a sharp chopping blade or a food chopper, chop the sauerkraut until it is very fine and equal in consistency to the chopped hot dogs. Add the chopped sauerkraut to the hot dog mixture. Cook over low heat, stirring frequently, until the mixture is thick and glossy. Remove from heat and cool to room temperature; then place in the coldest part of the refrigerator for at least 1 hour or until firm enough to form into firm balls.

Using the large end of a melon-ball maker, scoop up equal portions of the mixture and form into balls. Roll the balls in the ½ cup flour. Mix the eggs and cream together and dip each ball into it; then roll in the pretzel crumbs until evenly coated. Drop into vegetable oil which has been heated to 375° F. Fry for 5 minutes or until a rich golden brown. Drain on paper toweling. Insert a toothpick or cocktail pick into each ball for easier serving.

These appetizers can be made and fried in advance and then kept warm in the oven without impairing their flavor. Makes approximately 50 appetizers.

GLAZED HOT DOGS

8 hot dogs
1 tablespoon unflavored gelatin
2 tablespoons cold water
1 cup creamy-style French dressing
½ teaspoon salt
¼ teaspoon pepper
1 very large orange or grapefruit (optional)

Cut the hot dogs into 1-inch pieces crosswise and put a toothpick into the center of the 1-inch side of each piece of hot dog. Set aside on waxed paper.

Soak the gelatin in the cold water for 5 minutes or until softened. Place the softened gelatin in the top of a double boiler over rapidly boiling water. Cook over the hot water until the gelatin is completely dissolved. Add the cup of French dressing to the dissolved gelatin, stirring well. Add the salt and pepper. Remove from heat and allow the mixture to cool until it is slightly thickened.

Dip each hot dog piece into the thickened dressing; allow it to drip. Place the glazed hot dog pieces on a flat plate and chill in the refrigerator for about 1½ hours.

To serve, cut the orange or grapefruit in half, and place the halves cut side down on a serving platter. Stick the picks with the glazed hot dog pieces into the orange or grapefruit skin. The red-orange of the hot dogs and the orange or yellow of the fruit makes a very colorful dish. Makes about 30 appetizers.

HOT DOG AND OLIVE SPREAD

½ cup green, pimiento-stuffed olives, sliced 1/16 inch thick
8 hot dogs, finely chopped
½ cup mayonnaise
½ teaspoon powdered mustard
½ teaspoon celery seed

Mix all the ingredients thoroughly. Spread on 2-inch rounds of white bread. This is good as a cold appetizer. If you wish to serve hot, place the spread rounds of bread in the broiler about 4 inches away from the heat until the mixture is bubbly and just beginning to brown. Serve piping hot. Makes approximately 24 appetizers.

HOT DOGS IN EDAM FONDUE

8 hot dogs
1 Edam cheese (approximately ½ pound)
2 tablespoons brandy
1 teaspoon prepared yellow mustard
½ teaspoon horseradish
½ teaspoon Worcestershire sauce
⅛ teaspoon nutmeg
2 drops Tabasco

Cut the hot dogs into 1-inch pieces. Spear each hot dog piece with a colorful cocktail pick and place them in the bottom of a chafing dish or a candle-heated serving dish. Set aside, allowing the hot dogs to warm through.

Meanwhile, peel the wax coating from the ball of Edam cheese. Cut the cheese into wedges approximately ½ inch thick. Place the wedges in the top of a double boiler over very slowly boiling water. Cook until the cheese has melted, stirring occasionally.

After the cheese has melted, add the brandy, mustard, horseradish, Worcestershire sauce, nutmeg and Tabasco. Mix all well and pour over and around the hot dog pieces. Serve at once, keeping the cheese soft and melted over the chafing-dish burner or candle. Serve with rounds of Melba toast or toasted rounds of caraway rye bread. Makes about 36 appetizers.

PINK AND GOLD CLOVER LEAVES

½ cup mayonnaise
1 tablespoon prepared yellow mustard
32 cocktail crackers, approximately 2½ inches in diameter
8 slices American cheese, cut in quarters
4 hot dogs, cut in 8 slices per wiener

Mix the mustard and mayonnaise together well. Place a dab of mayonnaise in the center of each cracker. Place three slices of wiener clover-leaf fashion on top of the mayonnaise.

Place a quarter piece of the cheese on top of the hot dog slices. Put the crackers on a large cooky sheet; bake in a 400° F. oven until the cheese has melted. Serve at once, piping hot. Makes 32 hors d'oeuvres.

HOT DOG CANAPE #1

4 hot dogs
¼ cup grated Cheddar cheese
¼ cup condensed tomato soup
1 tablespoon grated onion
½ teaspoon horseradish
¼ teaspoon prepared mustard
1 tablespoon minced parsley
24 2-inch rounds toasted bread

Chop the hot dogs until they are the consistency of coarse corn meal. Add the Cheddar cheese, tomato soup, grated onion, horseradish, mustard and parsley. Blend all together until well mixed.

Spread on toasted bread rounds. Place on a cooky sheet; broil 6 inches from heat for 5 minutes or until the mixture begins to get bubbly and brown. Serve piping hot. Makes 24 canapes.

HOT DOG CANAPE #2

6 hot dogs
¾ cup grated sharp Cheddar cheese
¼ cup onion, finely chopped
1 egg, beaten until lemon yellow
1 teaspoon Dusseldorf-style prepared mustard
1 loaf snack rye bread

Chop the hot dogs until they are the consistency of coarse corn meal. Add the grated cheese, onion, beaten egg and mustard. Mix all thoroughly.

Spread the mixture on the slices of snack rye and place in a 375° F. oven for 15 minutes or until the cheese begins to melt and the tops are slightly browned and bubbly. Serve piping hot. Makes approximately 36 canapes.

HOT DOG OLIVES

30 very large pimiento-stuffed olives
3 hot dogs
1 3-ounce package cream cheese, at room temperature
1 drop Tabasco

Cut the stuffed olives in half lengthwise. Remove the pimiento stuffing and put in a chopping bowl along with the hot dogs. Chop the hot dogs and pimiento until the consistency of coarse corn meal.

Add the cream cheese to the hot dogs and pimiento. Mix together well. Add the Tabasco and mix again. Fill the olive halves with the mixture and fasten together with colored cocktail picks. Chill in the refrigerator for at least 1 hour before serving. Makes 30 appetizers.

HOT DOG SURPRISE #1

6 hot dogs
1 10-ounce can cream of celery soup
1 8-ounce package cream cheese, at room temperature
36 Melba toast rounds or cocktail rye slices

Chop the hot dogs until they are the consistency of coarse corn meal. Add the hot dogs and softened cream cheese to the condensed celery soup; mix thoroughly. Place in the refrigerator for 1 hour to firm up.

Spread the mixture on the Melba toast rounds; place on a cooky sheet. Broil 6 inches from heat until a delicate golden brown. Makes 36 appetizers.

HOT DOG SURPRISE #2

6 hot dogs
1 10-ounce can tomato soup
1 cup grated sharp Cheddar cheese
1 teaspoon horseradish, pressed dry
1 teaspoon prepared mustard
cocktail crackers

Chop the hot dogs until they are the consistency of coarse corn meal. Add the condensed tomato soup to the chopped hot dogs, then stir in the grated cheese, horseradish and mustard. Mix all well. Spread on cocktail crackers. Place on a cooky sheet; broil 6 inches from heat until they are a delicate shade of brown. Serve at once, piping hot. Makes 48 appetizers.

HOT DOG DOLLIES

12 slices lean bacon, about 10 inches in length
24 large pimiento-stuffed olives
8 hot dogs
24 round wooden picks
24 small sprigs parsley

Cut the bacon slices in half. Wrap each olive in a half slice of bacon so that the pimiento end is peeking out. Secure with one of the wooden picks by going through from the top to where the two ends of bacon overlap. Set aside.

Cut the hot dogs into thirds crosswise. On one cut end, make four cuts about 1 inch deep into the hot dog so that when it is set on this cut end, the four sections spread out like a skirt. Insert the bacon-wrapped olive in the uncut end. The "dolly" will stand up on the four skirt sections and the toothpick.

Place the dollies, standing upright, on a cooky sheet in a 400° F. oven for 10 minutes or until the bacon is crisp and golden. Insert the sprig of parsley where the bacon and the hot dog meet, like a bouquet.

These appetizers are good either hot or cold and create a real conversation piece at parties. If you want to be especially gay, insert an additional sprig of parsley in the bonnet of crisp bacon. Makes 24 dollies.

CUCUMBER INTRO

1 medium-sized cucumber
4 hot dogs, coarsely chopped
½ cup mayonnaise
1 tablespoon grated horseradish
1 tablespoon minced onion
1 teaspoon paprika

Using the saw-toothed edge of a potato peeler, score the sides of the cucumber leaving it half white and half green. Slice the cucumber into ¼-inch slices.

Mix the mayonnaise, horseradish and onion together. Put a dab of this flavored mayonnaise in the center of each cucumber slice; top the mayonnaise with some of the chopped hot dogs. Sprinkle with the paprika for color. Makes approximately 15 hors d'oeuvres.

DEVILED EGGS SUPREME

6 hard-boiled eggs, peeled and chilled
¼ cup mayonnaise
3 hot dogs, finely chopped
1 teaspoon Dusseldorf-style prepared mustard
6 pimiento-stuffed green olives, cut in half

Cut the eggs in half lengthwise; slip out the yolks and mash with a fork. Add the mayonnaise, the chopped hot dogs and the mustard; mix well.

Using a spatula, refill each egg white half with a heaping portion of the yolk mixture. Place one of the olive halves, pimiento side up, on the top of each egg. Chill in the refrigerator for 1 hour before serving.

If you want to be especially fancy, place the yolk mixture in a pastry tube with a serrated end. Force out the yolk mixture in a wavy design, and then top with the slice of olive. Makes 12 hors d'oeuvres.

PEANUT ROLL-UPS

6 slices fresh white enriched bread
6 hot dogs, cut in half horizontally
½ cup chunk-style peanut butter
½ cup Virginia-style peanuts, finely chopped
½ cup melted butter

Remove the crusts from the slices of bread. Cut the slices diagonally so that you end up with 12 triangles of bread. Spread each piece with peanut butter; sprinkle the chopped peanuts over the peanut butter.

Place a ½ hot dog on top of the peanuts and peanut butter. Bring up two corners of the bread and fasten them around the hot dog with a toothpick. Brush the outside of each roll-up with the melted butter. Broil about 6 inches from heat for 5 minutes or until the outside of the bread is a golden brown. Serve piping hot. Makes 12 hors d'oeuvres.

DOGGIE PUFFS

1 cup boiling water
½ cup soft butter
¼ teaspoon salt
1 cup all-purpose flour
4 eggs
8 hot dogs
¼ cup hot dog mustard relish
1 tablespoon onion, finely chopped
1 tablespoon dehydrated parsley

Bring the water to a rolling boil and add the soft butter. Continue cooking for 1 minute longer or until all of the butter has melted. Remove from heat and allow to cool slightly.

Mix the salt with the flour and add to the butter-water mixture. Beat with a slotted spoon until smooth. Add the eggs, one at a time; beat vigorously after each addition. Drop by spoonfuls, in circles about the size of a quarter, onto a lightly greased cooky sheet. Leave about a ¾-inch space between each circle. Bake in a 350° F. oven for 25 minutes or until they are just slightly browned and puffed up.

Chop the hot dogs until they are about the same consistency as the hot dog mustard relish. Add the chopped onion and parsley and mix all well with the relish.

Halve each puff horizontally and place about a teaspoonful of the hot dog mixture in the center of the bottom half. Replace the top and return the puffs to the cooky sheet. Place in a 400° F. oven for 3 minutes or until the tops are a rich golden brown. Serve at once. Makes about 40 appetizers.

Chapter III

HOT DOG SOUPS

WHEN YOU LOOK at hot dogs with cold logic, there is no reason why they shouldn't augment the flavors of soup. After all, they are pure meat, delicately flavored, with nary a speck of waste.

Every soup does not lend itself to using hot dogs, but there are many that do. Some soups are just too strongly flavored and overwhelm the hot dogs. The blander flavored soups seem to be most compatible with hot dogs.

Try some of the recipes in this chapter if you've never "souped up" a hot dog. Then start experimenting with some of your own favorite soup recipes—you will be pleasantly surprised.

The soups in this chapter are all "made from scratch." However, hot dogs can be added to many of the wonderful canned soups one finds on the supermarket shelves. If you are a canned soup fan for those hurry-up lunches, try adding hot dogs the next time. This is an excellent way to up the protein content and enhance the flavor of the soup. Active children with their innate love of hot dogs will especially enjoy the addition.

POLISH BREAD SOUP WITH HOT DOGS

6 cups hot beef stock
6 slices enriched white bread, toasted lightly
6 eggs, poached until just firm
6 hot dogs, cut in ¼-inch slices

The soup stock in this recipe would be seasoned to taste and boiling hot.

Place a slice of the toast in the bottom of each soup bowl. Place a poached egg on top of the toast, and distribute a portion of the hot dog slices around the edge of the bread.

Pour 1 cup of the boiling hot soup stock over the toast, egg and hot dog pieces. Serve at once. Serves 6.

BEAN SOUP WITH HOT DOGS

1 cup dried Navy beans, soaked overnight in water to cover
1 ham bone from the hock end of a ham
1½ quarts water
6 whole cloves
6 whole allspice
6 peppercorns
1 clove garlic, sliced paper thin
1 cup onion, coarsely chopped
½ teaspoon salt
½ cup sliced, pitted ripe olives
8 hot dogs, cut in ½-inch circles
¼ cup parsley, finely chopped

Drain the soaked beans and rinse under cold running water. Place the beans and the ham bone in a 3-quart soup kettle. Add the water. Place the cloves, allspice, peppercorns and garlic slices in a little cloth bag and add to the beans and the hambone. Add the chopped onion and salt. Cook over moderate heat for 2 hours or until the beans mash easily against the side of the kettle.

Remove the bag of spices and the ham bone and discard. Strain the soup through a coarse sieve. Force half of the beans through the sieve and return the remainder to the soup stock.

Add the sliced olives and the hot dog circles. Place over moderate heat for 8 minutes longer, to warm the hot dog pieces thoroughly. Stir in the chopped parsley just before serving. Serve with saltines or croutons. Serves 6.

CORN CHOWDER WITH HOT DOGS

½ cup diced bacon
½ cup diced onion
1 cup water
1 cup raw potatoes, peeled and diced
1 #2 can creamed corn
2 cups milk
4 hot dogs, diced in ¼-inch cubes

Saute the bacon in the bottom of a soup kettle until it is a golden brown. Add the onion and continue to saute until it is transparent and tender. Pour off any excess bacon fat. Add the water and the potatoes and bring to a rolling boil. Turn the heat down to simmer and continue to cook for 15 minutes or until the edges of the potato are transparent.

Add the creamed corn and milk. Simmer for an additional 8 minutes, stirring occasionally to prevent sticking. Add the hot dog cubes just before serving. Serve with saltines. Serves 4.

KIDNEY BEAN SOUP WITH HOT DOGS

2 #2 cans red kidney beans
1½ cups Burgundy wine
1 cup sliced onion
¼ teaspoon ground cloves
½ teaspoon salt
¼ teaspoon pepper
½ teaspoon Accent
1 cup warm water
6 hot dogs, cut in ⅛-inch circles
2 tablespoons parsley, very finely chopped
6 slices enriched white bread
½ teaspoon savory
½ cup melted butter

Drain the kidney beans and place their liquid in a large saucepan along with the Burgundy wine and the sliced onion. Stir in the ground cloves, salt, pepper and Accent. Simmer over low heat for 8 minutes.

Meanwhile puree the kidney beans in a food blender or force them through a fine sieve.

Strain the bean liquid and wine mixture and return to the saucepan. Discard the onions. Add the pureed beans, sliced hot dogs and water. Simmer for an additional 8 minutes.

Brush both sides of the bread with the melted butter and then sprinkle lightly with the savory. Stack the bread slices together and cut up into ½-inch cubes. Spread the buttered bread cubes over the bottom of a shallow baking pan and place in a 450° F. oven for 10 minutes or until they are a golden brown. Stir the parsley into the hot soup and serve piping hot with the toasted croutons. Serves 6.

POTATO SOUP WITH HOT DOGS #1

2 cups raw potatoes, peeled and diced in ½-inch cubes
2 cups onions, diced in ½-inch cubes
2 beef bouillon cubes
½ teaspoon salt
¼ teaspoon pepper
2 cups milk, scalded
1 cup half-and-half cream, scalded along with the milk
3 tablespoons dehydrated parsley
6 hot dogs, cut in ¼-inch circles

Place the diced potatoes and diced onions in a saucepan with enough water to cover. Cook over moderate heat until the potatoes are fork tender. Drain off 1 cup of the potato water and dissolve the bouillon cubes in it. Discard the remainder of the potato stock.

Force the boiled potatoes and onions through a coarse sieve and then add the bouillon water to them; add the salt and pepper and mix well. Gradually stir this mixture into the scalded milk and half-and-half cream.

Place over very low heat; stir in the parsley and the sliced hot dogs; heat for 5 more minutes. Serve piping hot with oyster crackers. Serves 6.

POTATO SOUP WITH HOT DOGS #2

6 hot dogs, cut in ½-inch circles
6 medium-sized Idaho potatoes
3 cups cold water
½ cup flour
4 cups milk
1 teaspoon salt
¼ teaspoon pepper
½ teaspoon pulverized thyme
⅛ teaspoon oregano
½ cup butter
3 cups onion, finely chopped
1 cup half-and-half cream
¼ cup cooking sherry

Peel the potatoes and dice them into ½-inch cubes. Place in a kettle with the cold water and bring to a boil over moderate heat. Cook until the edges are transparent and glazed. Remove from heat and mash the potatoes coarsely in their liquid.

Mix the flour and milk together until smoothly blended. Add to the potato mixture along with the salt, pepper, thyme and oregano. Mix all well and place over very low heat, stirring frequently to prevent sticking. Cook for 8 minutes or until slightly thickened.

Place the butter in a saucepan over moderate heat. When melted, add the chopped onion and cook until onion is limp and transparent. Add the onion and its butter to the potato mixture.

Add the half-and-half; add the sherry, stirring rapidly to prevent curdling. Add the hot dog circles and continue to cook over very low heat for an additional 5 minutes or until the hot dogs are heated through. Serves 6 generously.

BEAN AND HOT DOG CHOWDER

6 hot dogs, cut in ¼-inch slices
2 tablespoons butter or margarine
½ cup celery, diagonally sliced ⅛ inch thick
¾ cup onion, thinly sliced
¼ cup green pepper, finely chopped
2 #300 cans pork and beans (approximately 3½ cups)
2 8-ounce cans tomato sauce
½ teaspoon salt
¼ teaspoon pepper
1 teaspoon brown sugar

Place the sliced hot dogs and margarine in a large soup kettle over moderate heat. Saute the hot dogs until they just begin to get brown. Add the celery, onion and green pepper and continue to saute until the onion is limp and transparent.

Remove the pieces of pork from the beans and discard. Add the beans, juice and all, to the hot dog mixture. Continue to cook over moderate heat. Add the tomato sauce, salt, pepper and brown sugar and mix all well. Cook for 5 to 8 minutes longer or until all is heated through.

Serve in bowls, just as you would thick chili con carne. Serve with saltines. Serves 6.

PEA SOUP WITH HOT DOGS

2 cups dried peas
1 large ham bone
12 cups water
½ teaspoon salt
¼ teaspoon pepper
2 cups diced celery
2 cups onions, thinly sliced
1 cup raw potatoes, peeled and diced
¼ cup parsley, finely chopped
8 hot dogs, cut in ⅛-inch circles

Soak the peas overnight in cold water to cover. The next day, drain away the water in which the peas were soaked. Place the peas, ham bone, water, salt and pepper in a soup kettle with a tightly fitting cover. Bring to a rolling boil and skim off any froth which may gather.

Add the celery, onions, potatoes and parsley. Again bring to a rolling boil, then reduce the heat to simmer. Cook for 1 hour or until the peas can be crushed against the side of the kettle.

Remove the ham bone and discard, then puree the soup by forcing through a fine sieve. Return the pureed soup to the heat and add the hot dogs. Cook for an additional 5 minutes. Serve piping hot with saltines or croutons. Serves 6.

SPLIT PEA SOUP WITH HOT DOGS

1 cup quick-cook split peas
4 cups water
1 large bay leaf
½ cup celery, diced in ¼-inch cubes
1 carrot, finely shredded
½ cup onion, diced in ¼-inch cubes
1 clove garlic, cut in half
¼ cup butter
1 teaspoon salt
¼ teaspoon pepper
1½ cups milk
8 hot dogs

Place the quick-cook split peas in a 2½-quart saucepan with the water, bay leaf, celery, carrot, onion and garlic.

Cook over low heat for 40 minutes or until the peas can be mashed against the side of the kettle with ease.

Remove the bay leaf and the two pieces of garlic. Strain the mixture through a sieve, and then force the peas and vegetables through the sieve. Add the butter, salt, pepper and milk.

Mix well and place over very low heat. Cut the hot dogs into quarters the long way, and then cut in half crosswise. Add the hot dog pieces to the soup and continue to cook over very low heat for 5 minutes longer or until piping hot. Serve with croutons. Serves 6.

GERMAN BEEF AND HOT DOG SOUP

1½ pounds beef stew meat, cut in 1-inch cubes
1 tablespoon paprika
2 tablespoons butter
2 cups onion, diced in ½-inch cubes
6 cups water
1 teaspoon salt
¼ teaspoon pepper
1 #303 can tomatoes (2 cups)
3 cups raw potatoes, peeled and diced in ½-inch cubes
6 hot dogs, cut in ½-inch slices
2 tablespoons parsley, finely chopped

Sprinkle the beef cubes with the paprika. Melt the butter in the bottom of a large soup kettle which has a tightly fitting cover. Add the beef cubes and saute them until they are a rich brown color.

Add the diced onion and continue to saute until the onion is transparent and tender. Add the water, salt, pepper and tomatoes. Cover tightly and simmer for 1 hour or until the beef is tender enough to cut with a fork.

Add the diced raw potatoes and cook for 15 minutes or until the edges of the potatoes are transparent and they are fork tender. If the soup has become too thick, add a little more water.

Add the hot dog slices and cook for 5 minutes longer. Serve at once, piping hot. Garnish each bowl with a sprinkle of parsley. Serve with saltines. Serves 6.

HOT DOG AND ONION SOUP

6 hot dogs
2 tablespoons butter
2 cups sweet onion, sliced 1/8 inch thick
1/4 cup grated carrot
2 tablespoons all-purpose flour
4 beef bouillon cubes, dissolved in 2 cups boiling water
1/4 teaspoon pepper
1 1/2 cups half-and-half cream, heated to just below the
  boiling point

Melt the butter in a 2-quart saucepan. Add the chopped onion and grated carrot. Saute over low heat until the onion becomes transparent and soft. Stir in the flour and blend until smooth. Add the 2 cups of boiling water with the bouillon cubes dissolved in it. Cover tightly and simmer for 35 minutes.

Cut the hot dogs into 1/4-inch slices; add to the simmering bouillon and onion. Cook for 6 minutes longer. Take several spoonfuls of the bouillon mixture and stir into the hot cream, then add the hot cream to the bouillon mixture. Add pepper. Mix well and serve piping hot. Serve with saltines. Serves 6.

HOT DOG BARLEY SOUP

8 hot dogs, cut in 1/8-inch circles
2/3 cup barley
6 cups water
1/2 teaspoon salt
1/4 teaspoon pepper
3/4 cup carrots, diced in 1/4-inch cubes
3/4 cup onion, diced in 1/4-inch cubes
3/4 cup turnip, diced in 1/4-inch cubes
3/4 cup celery, diced in 1/4-inch cubes
1/4 cup parsley, finely chopped

Place the hot dog slices, barley and water in a saucepan with a tightly fitting cover. Cook over moderate heat for 20 minutes.

Add the salt, pepper, carrots, onion, turnip, celery and parsley and continue to cook over moderate heat for another

40 minutes or until the carrots are soft and tender. Serve piping hot with saltines. Serves 4. (If this soup is too thick for your family's tastes, a little hot water may be added.)

QUICK HOT DOG SOUP

8 hot dogs, diced in ¼-inch cubes
2 tablespoons butter
2 tablespoons onion, finely chopped
1 10-ounce can cream of celery soup
1 10-ounce can cream of chicken soup
2 cups mashed potatoes; these can be leftovers or the instant type prepared according to package directions
2 cups milk
½ teaspoon salt
¼ teaspoon pepper
½ cup chopped water cress or ½ cup chopped fresh spinach

Melt the butter in a 2-quart saucepan over moderate heat. Add the chopped onion and saute until the onion is limp and transparent. Add the celery and chicken soup. Mix all well.

Stir in the mashed potatoes and add the milk. Again mix all well. Add the salt and pepper and cook over very low heat for 10 minutes or until the mixture is steaming hot, stirring frequently.

Add the hot dog cubes and the chopped water cress. Continue to cook for 3 minutes longer or until the hot dogs are heated through. Do not cover during this last 3 minutes of cooking or the bright green of the water cress or spinach will be lost.

Serve piping hot with saltines. Serves 6.

HOT DOG LENTIL SOUP

1 large ham bone or 2 cups diced lean ham
8 cups cold water
1 cup lentils
1 cup celery, diced in ¼-inch cubes
1 cup onion, diced in ¼-inch cubes
1 bay leaf
½ teaspoon salt
6 peppercorns
2 tablespoons cider vinegar
8 wieners, cut in ⅛-inch circles

Place the ham bone or ham in a large soup kettle with a tightly fitting cover. Add the water, lentils, celery, onion, bay leaf, salt and peppercorns and bring to a rolling boil. Turn the heat back to simmer and cook for 1½ hours or until the lentils can be crushed against the side of the kettle.

Stir in the cider vinegar and the wieners and cook for an additional 5 minutes. Serve piping hot with saltines. Serves 6.

Chapter IV

SALADS MADE WITH HOT DOGS

SINCE ALL HOT DOGS are completely cooked when you purchase them at your supermarket, isn't it a good idea to use them in salads? If you're tired of adding canned fish or cold chicken or ham to your salads, try adding hot dogs. Not only are they far more economical, but the new taste will please everyone who tries it.

Salads made with hot dogs are a natural for summertime feasting. In summer, most of us are more active than in winter and protein is needed to sustain muscles. You can become a first-class "protein sneaker" if you make your salads with delicious, economical hot dogs. Children who are sometimes very adept at skipping vegetables will become avid salad eaters if you perk those salads up with the addition of hot dogs.

This chapter contains both hearty he-man salads and lighter ones. Again we urge you to experiment by using hot dogs in your own favorite salad recipes.

HOT DOG SHOESTRING SALAD

10 hot dogs
¼ cup onion, finely chopped
1½ cups celery, finely chopped
¼ cup grated raw carrots
¾ cup salad dressing or mayonnaise
1 large can shoestring potatoes
6 large lettuce leaves

Cut the hot dogs up into thirds and then cut each third into shoestring-sized strips. Place the shoestring hot dogs in a mixing bowl which has a tightly fitting cover. Add the onion, celery, carrots and half of the salad dressing. Toss to mix and chill in the refrigerator for at least a ½ hour.

When ready to serve, add the remainder of the salad dressing, the can of shoestring potatoes and again toss to mix. Place a portion of the salad on each of the lettuce leaves. Serves 6.

TOSSED HOT DOG SALAD

10 hot dogs
1 medium-sized head iceberg lettuce
¾ cup chopped tart apple, cored but not peeled
½ cup dill pickle, diced in ¼-inch cubes
¾ cup pitted, sliced ripe olives
¼ cup mayonnaise
¼ cup dairy sour cream
1 teaspoon lemon juice

Slice each hot dog into quarters the long way and then cut the quarters in half crosswise. Each hot dog will yield 8 strips. Break the lettuce up into bite-sized pieces and place in a large salad bowl along with the hot dog strips, the apple, dill pickle and the sliced ripe olives.

Whip the mayonnaise, sour cream and lemon juice together until light and fluffy. Add to the salad greens and the hot dogs. Toss all lightly and serve. Serves 6.

Variations:

Use French dressing instead of mayonnaise for a nippier flavor.
Garnish with 4 hard-boiled, sliced eggs for added flavor.
Add 1 tablespoon drained capers for a flavor variation.
Add ¾ cup American cheese cut in ¼-inch cubes for flavor variation.
Add ¾ cup commercial croutons at the last minute for crunchiness.

REFRIGERATOR HOT DOG AND POTATO SALAD

12 medium-sized salad potatoes
12 hot dogs
2 tablespoons vinegar
1 tablespoon water
¼ teaspoon celery seed
1 tablespoon onion juice
½ teaspoon salt
¼ teaspoon pepper
¼ cup mayonnaise
6 lettuce cups

Cook the unpeeled salad potatoes in slightly salted water until they are tender enough to be pierced with a fork. Drain and peel. Slice the potatoes while still hot into ¼-inch slices. Slice the hot dogs into ¼-inch slices and toss lightly with the potato slices.

Mix the vinegar, water, celery seed, onion juice, salt and pepper together. Drizzle this mixture over the potatoes and hot dogs. Turn the mixture over several times so that the flavors are evenly distributed. When cooled to room temperature, cover tightly and place in the refrigerator for at least 2 hours to chill thoroughly.

Before serving add the mayonnaise and mix well. Serve in lettuce cups. Garnish with sprigs of parsley or strips of pimiento for added color. Serves 6.

HOT DOG APPLE SALAD

2 cups elbow macaroni, cooked according to package directions
6 hot dogs
4 medium-sized McIntosh Apples
2 tablespoons lemon juice
4 stalks pascal celery
1 tablespoon onion, finely chopped
1 teaspoon celery seed
¼ cup parsley, finely chopped
1 cup dairy sour cream
½ teaspoon salt
1 teaspoon prepared mustard
6 lettuce cups

Drain the macaroni and set aside. Cut the hot dogs up into ¼-inch cubes. Add to the macaroni and mix well.

Peel and core the apples. Cut up into ½-inch cubes. Drench with lemon juice and set aside for 5 minutes; then add to the macaroni mixture. Cut the celery diagonally into 1/16-inch slices. Add to the macaroni mixture. Add the chopped onion, celery seed and the parsley. Mix all well.

In a separate bowl, mix the sour cream, salt and mustard until well blended. Pour this mixture over the hot dog-macaroni mixture. Turn the mixture over several times until all is well mixed and evenly flavored. Chill in the refrigerator for at least 2 hours. Serve in lettuce cups. Serves 6.

HOT DOG ASPIC

1 tablespoon unflavored gelatin
¼ cup cold water
1½ cups hot beef bouillon or stock
10 hot dogs
½ cup celery, diced in ¼-inch cubes
¼ cup parsley, finely chopped
5 hard-boiled eggs, chilled and peeled
shredded lettuce

Soften the gelatin in the ¼ cup cold water. Dissolve the softened gelatin in the hot beef stock. Stir well until all of the gelatin granules are dissolved.

Cut the hot dogs in half and stand them on end, cut side down, in a 10-inch circular tube mold. Sprinkle the diced celery and the parsley over the bottom of the mold.

Cut the hard-boiled eggs lengthwise and place them around the center "tube" of the mold. Pour the gelatin mixture carefully into the mold.

Place in the refrigerator for at least 4 hours. Unmold on a bed of shredded lettuce. Serve in generous slices. Serves 6.

HOT DOG AND MACARONI SALAD #1

2 cups elbow macaroni, cooked according to package directions
1 8-inch cucumber
½ cup chopped onion
½ cup chopped green pepper
½ cup chopped celery
8 hot dogs, cut in ½-inch cubes
½ teaspoon salt
¼ teaspoon pepper
¼ teaspoon paprika
2 cups mayonnaise
4 hard-boiled eggs, peeled and sliced

Drain and rinse the macaroni in cold running water. Set aside to drain thoroughly.

Scrape the sides of the cucumber with a sharp fork or with the saw-tooth side of a potato peeler, removing just a portion of the peeling. Remove the cucumber ends and slice lengthwise into quarters. Using a teaspoon, scrape away the seeds and pulp and discard. Cut the cucumber into 1/8-inch pieces.

Add the cucumber pieces to the drained macaroni; add the onion, green pepper, celery and hot dogs. Mix all lightly.

Add the salt, pepper and paprika to the mayonnaise. Dice two of the sliced eggs and add to the mayonnaise. Reserve the other two sliced eggs for garnish. Add the mayonnaise to the macaroni-hot dog mixture. Fold and mix lightly. Place in a large serving bowl and garnish the top with slices of egg. Chill in the refrigerator at least 2 hours before serving. Serves 6 generously.

HOT DOG AND MACARONI SALAD #2

1 cup elbow macaroni, cooked according to package directions
1 cup American cheese, cut in 1/4-inch cubes
1/2 cup celery, diced in 1/4-inch pieces
1 canned pimiento, cut in 1/4-inch pieces
1/4 cup green pepper, diced in 1/4-inch cubes
8 hot dogs, diced in 1/4-inch cubes
1 cup mayonnaise
2 teaspoons cider vinegar
1 teaspoon Worcestershire sauce
1 tablespoon chopped parsley
6 lettuce cups

Rinse the cooked macaroni under cold running water and allow to drain thoroughly.

Place the drained macaroni in a mixing bowl; add the cubed cheese, celery, pimiento, green pepper and diced hot dogs. Mix all thoroughly.

Mix the mayonnaise, vinegar, Worcestershire sauce and parsley together well. Pour this mixture over the hot dog and macaroni mixture. Fold together with a light hand.

Place a portion of the salad in each of the lettuce cups. Chill in the refrigerator for 1/2 hour and serve. Serves 6.

FRESH SPINACH SALAD WITH HOT DOGS

1 pound fresh spinach, washed and thoroughly drained
2 cups cabbage, finely chopped
1 orange, peeled, seeded and sliced ¼ inch thick
¾ cup celery, diagonally sliced ⅛ inch thick
1 tablespoon grated onion
1 tablespoon parsley, finely chopped
1 tablespoon green pepper, finely chopped
⅓ cup salad oil
¼ cup cider vinegar
½ teaspoon salt
⅛ teaspoon pepper
8 hot dogs, diced in ¼-inch cubes

Using a kitchen shears, cut the spinach into ¼-inch ribbons. Add the cabbage and the sliced orange segments. Toss lightly to mix.

Mix the celery, onion, parsley, green pepper, salad oil, vinegar, salt and pepper together. Pour over the spinach and cabbage. Add the diced hot dogs and toss all lightly so that the salad ingredients are coated with the salad oil, vinegar and seasonings. Serves 6.

Variation:

Eliminate the oil and vinegar and use ½ cup French dressing instead.

HOT DOG AND FOUR BEAN SALAD

1 #303 can green beans, undrained
1 #303 can yellow wax beans, undrained
1 #303 can green lima beans, drained
1 #303 can red kidney beans, drained
½ cup onion, thinly sliced
½ cup green pepper, diced in ¼-inch cubes
6 hot dogs, diced in ¼-inch cubes
1 cup cider vinegar
1½ cups granulated sugar
½ cup peanut oil

Place the green beans and their liquid and the wax beans

36

and their liquid in a large mixing bowl which has a tightly fitting cover.

After draining the lima beans and the kidney beans, rinse them well under cold running water to eliminate all of the cloudy liquid. Let them drain in a collander until completely free of liquid and then add them to the other beans in the mixing bowl. Add the onion, green pepper and the diced hot dogs. Set aside.

Place the vinegar and the sugar in a saucepan and bring to a rolling boil for 2 minutes. Remove from the heat and add the peanut oil. Pour this mixture over the mixture of beans and hot dogs. Mix all well and chill in the refrigerator, tightly covered, for 2 hours. Serves 6 generously.

Note: This is an excellent salad for buffet suppers or for cookouts because it can be made the day before and still taste delicious.

HOT DOG AND LENTIL SALAD

1½ cups lentils, cooked according to package directions
½ cup red Italian onion, thinly sliced
½ cup cubed tart baking apple; cored but unpeeled
¼ cup canned pimiento, cut in ¼-inch cubes
½ cup celery, cut in ¼-inch cubes
8 hot dogs, cut in ¼-inch circles
¼ cup fresh lemon juice
½ cup salad oil
¼ teaspoon black pepper
¼ teaspoon powdered mustard
2 tablespoons dehydrated parsley
12 large sprigs of water cress or 6 lettuce cups

Drain the cooked lentils and allow them to cool to room temperature. Add the sliced onion, cubed apple, pimiento and celery. Add the sliced hot dogs and toss all lightly to mix well.

Mix the lemon juice, salad oil, black pepper, mustard and parsley together well. Pour this mixture over the other ingredients and mix lightly.

Cover and place in the refrigerator for at least 4 hours or overnight. Serve on the sprigs of water cress or in a lettuce cup. Serves 6.

MIXED UP HOT DOG SALAD #1

1 8-inch diameter cauliflower (it should be young and tender)
6 hot dogs, diced in ¼-inch cubes
1 clove garlic, finely minced
1 3-inch diameter Bermuda onion, cut in ⅛-inch slices
½ cup green pepper, diced in ¼-inch pieces
1 canned pimiento, cut in ¼-inch pieces
¾ cup pitted green olives, cut in ⅛-inch slices
3 cups shredded iceberg lettuce
1 cup French dressing
¾ cup crumbled blue cheese

Soak the cauliflower in slightly salted cold water for about 2 hours. Drain, then break up the cauliflower into bite-sized pieces. If there are any thick stems, dice them into ¼-inch pieces.

Place the cauliflower pieces, diced hot dogs, garlic, onion slices, green pepper and pimiento in a large salad bowl. Add the sliced olives and the shredded lettuce and toss all very lightly.

Mix the French dressing and the blue cheese thoroughly. Drizzle the dressing over the salad greens. Chill in the refrigerator for 30 minutes before serving. Serves 6 generously.

MIXED UP HOT DOG SALAD #2

8 hot dogs
6 slices Italian salami, ⅛ inch thick
1 medium-sized head lettuce
6 strips of bacon, cut in ¼-inch cubes
¼ cup cider vinegar
1 teaspoon sugar
1 cup hot boiled potatoes, peeled and diced in ½-inch cubes

Dice the hot dogs and the salami into ¼-inch cubes. Break the lettuce up into bite-sized pieces. Mix the lettuce, hot dog cubes and salami cubes together by tossing lightly.

Place the bacon in a skillet and saute until it is crisp and brown. Using a slotted spoon, remove the bacon pieces from the fat and add them to the salad greens.

Add the vinegar and sugar to the bacon fat and simmer over very low heat for 3 minutes.

Pour the hot vinegar and bacon dripping mixture over the salad ingredients. Add the hot diced potatoes and toss all lightly. Serve at once. Serves 6.

Variations:

Substitute Thuringer sausage for the Italian salami.
Add ½ cup commercial croutons to the salad at the last minute for added flavor and crunchiness.

KIDNEY BEAN SALAD WITH HOT DOGS

1 1-pound can kidney beans
2 cups celery, finely chopped
½ cup chopped sweet pickle relish
1 tablespoon grated onion
2 hard-boiled eggs, coarsely chopped
2 tablespoons fresh lemon juice
½ teaspoon salt
1½ teaspoons prepared yellow mustard
8 hot dogs, diced in ½-inch cubes
6 lettuce cups

Drain the kidney beans and rinse under cold running water. Drain again and set aside.

Mix the celery, pickle relish, grated onion, chopped eggs, lemon juice, salt, mustard and diced hot dogs together. Add the drained kidney beans. Mix well and place in the refrigerator for at least 1 hour before serving.

Place a portion of the salad in each of the lettuce cups and serve. Serves 6.

Variations:

Substitute a 1-pound can of yellow butter beans for the kidney beans.
Substitute 2 tablespoons vinegar for the lemon juice.
Mix the chopped egg whites into the salad; reserve the chopped yolks for a garnish over each portion.
If you like a thicker salad, do not rinse the kidney beans, but just drain them slightly.

HOT DOG AND BEAN SALAD #1

6 hot dogs, diced in ¼-inch cubes
1 #2 can French-cut green beans, drained
1 #2 can French-cut yellow wax beans, drained
1 #2 can chick peas, drained and rinsed with cold water
1 5-ounce can water chestnuts, drained and thinly sliced
2 red Italian onions or 1 large Bermuda onion; peeled, sliced ¼ inch thick and separated into rings
½ cup cider vinegar
½ cup granulated sugar
1 teaspoon Accent
¼ cup olive oil
3 tablespoons soy sauce
1 teaspoon celery seed
½ teaspoon paprika

Place the hot dog pieces, the green beans, the wax beans, chick peas, water chestnuts and onion rings in a large bowl and toss gently so that all the ingredients are evenly mixed.

In your blender or in a fruit jar, place the vinegar, sugar, Accent, olive oil, soy sauce, celery seed and paprika. Blend or shake for a few minutes so that all the ingredients are thoroughly mixed. Pour over the salad ingredients. Chill in the refrigerator at least 2 hours, turning the salad ingredients over several times so that all the flavors unite. Serves 8.

HOT DOG AND BEAN SALAD #2

6 hot dogs, diced in ¼-inch cubes
2 1-pound cans pork and beans
2 cups pascal celery, diagonally sliced
¼ cup diced green pepper
½ teaspoon salt
¼ teaspoon seasoned pepper (available in spice section of most supermarkets)
4 tablespoons lemon juice
6 to 8 large lettuce leaves
3 medium-sized red Italian onions, peeled, sliced ¼ inch thick and separated into rings

Mix the diced hot dogs with the pork and beans. Add the pascal celery and the green pepper. Add the salt, seasoned pepper and the lemon juice. Mix all together lightly so the beans do not become crushed.

Arrange the lettuce leaves around the outer edge of a large salad bowl, then arrange the rings of onion on top of the lettuce. Pour the bean salad mixture into the middle. Chill in the refrigerator for at least an hour. Serves 8.

POTATO SALAD AND HOT DOG STICKS

12 hot dogs
12 2-inch diameter salad potatoes, cooked, peeled and
   sliced (about 6 cups)
½ cup pascal celery, diced in ¼-inch cubes
6 green onions, sliced paper thin (use a little of the
   green too)
½ teaspoon salt
½ teaspoon celery salt
¼ cup radishes, thinly sliced
1 16-ounce carton dairy sour cream
¼ cup French dressing
1 drop Tabasco
3 hard-boiled eggs, peeled and sliced
1 tablespoon parsley, finely chopped

Place the hot dogs in a saucepan with cold water to cover. Place over moderate heat until the water barely reaches the boiling point. Remove from the heat and let stand for 5 minutes. Drain and slice each hot dog into quarters lengthwise and then cut in half crosswise, ending up with 8 "sticks" per hot dog. If you cut them while they are hot they will curl backwards, making a more decorative dish. Place the cut-up hot dogs in the refrigerator to chill.

Mix the sliced potatoes, celery, green onions, salt, celery salt and radishes together lightly. Mix the sour cream, French dressing and Tabasco together thoroughly. Pour this over the potato mixture and again mix lightly so that all of the potato slices are covered with the dressing. Chill in the refrigerator at least 2 hours.

Arrange the chilled hot dog sticks around the outside of a platter. Place the chilled potato salad in the middle and garnish with slices of egg. Sprinkle the parsley over all. Serves 6.

HOT GERMAN POTATO SALAD AND HOT DOGS

3 cups cooked, peeled salad potatoes, sliced ¼ inch thick
12 hot dogs
6 slices lean bacon
¼ cup juice from sweet and sour pickles
¼ cup vinegar
4 tablespoons granulated sugar
¼ teaspoon powdered mustard
½ teaspoon salt
¼ teaspoon pepper
3 tablespoons flour
½ cup water
½ onion, diced in ¼-inch cubes
½ cup celery, diced in ¼-inch cubes

Cut the hot dogs up into ¼-inch slices and mix lightly with the potato slices. Set aside.

Dice the bacon into ¼-inch pieces and place in a large oven-proof skillet. Saute the bacon until it is crisp and golden. Lower the heat and add the pickle juice, vinegar, sugar, powdered mustard, salt and pepper. Simmer for 2 minutes.

Mix the flour with the half cup of water until it is smooth and add to the bacon mixture. Stir well and continue to simmer for a few minutes longer until the mixture has thickened and become somewhat transparent. Add the potatoes and hot dogs, onion and celery. Turn the entire mixture over several times so that the dressing is evenly distributed. Place in a 300° F. oven for 15 minutes or until warmed through. Serve at once. Serves 6.

WILTED LETTUCE MADE WITH HOT DOGS

1 pound leaf lettuce (this is usually sold in fan-like bunches, but have it weighed so that you have approximately 1 pound)
1 cup celery, diagonally sliced ⅛ inch thick
½ cup onion, finely chopped
1 cup white radishes, thinly sliced (white is preferred, but you can use red)
3 tablespoons butter
2 tablespoons granulated sugar
¼ cup cider vinegar
¼ cup water
1 tablespoon cornstarch
6 strips bacon, cut in ½-inch pieces
4 hot dogs, cut in ½-inch cubes
4 medium-sized potatoes, peeled and boiled until tender
4 hard-boiled eggs, peeled and sliced
4 additional hot dogs, cut in half lengthwise

Wash the lettuce and dry it well. Using a shears, snip the lettuce up into 1-inch strips. Toss together lightly with the onion, celery, and radishes.

Melt the butter in a saucepan. Stir in the vinegar and sugar. Mix the water with the cornstarch and add to the vinegar mixture. Cook over low heat until it is thickened and transparent.

Saute the bacon until it is crisp and golden; pour off half of the fat and discard. Add the hot dog cubes and saute until slightly browned. Add the vinegar mixture to the hot dog-bacon mixture; cook over low heat for a few seconds.

Drain the potatoes and break them up with a fork. They should not be mashed, but left in uneven lumps. Add the potato pieces to the lettuce, and then pour the hot vinegar-bacon-hot dog mixture over the lettuce and potatoes. Mix well; turn the entire salad over in the bowl several times so that the flavors are well blended.

Place mixture in a salad bowl. Decorate the top with the slices of egg. Place the hot dog halves around the outside edge. Serves 6.

JELLIED HOT DOG LOAF

12 hot dogs
1 tablespoon unflavored gelatin
¼ cup cold water
1 cup boiling water
¼ cup fresh lemon juice
½ cup sweet-sour pickles, very finely sliced
½ cup pimiento-stuffed olives, very finely sliced
1 tablespoon onion, finely grated
1 teaspoon prepared Dusseldorf-style mustard
½ cup mayonnaise

Chop six of the hot dogs until they are the consistency of coarse corn meal. Set aside.

Soften the gelatin in the cold water for 5 minutes. Add the hot water and stir until all of the gelatin is completely dissolved. Add the lemon juice. Place in the coldest part of the refrigerator for 1 hour or until thickened.

Beat the thickened gelatin with an electric or rotary beater until it is light and fluffy. Fold in the chopped hot dogs, pickles, olives, grated onion, mustard and mayonnaise.

Place three of the whole hot dogs in the bottom of a loaf pan which has been rinsed in ice cold water. Pour one half of the gelatin mixture over them. Place the remaining three hot dogs over the gelatin. Pour the remainder of the gelatin mixture over them. Place in the coldest part of the refrigerator for at least 4 hours.

Unmold on a thick bed of shredded lettuce. Slice in generous slices and serve with additional mayonnaise which has been slightly flavored with horseradish. Serves 6.

IN THE PINK POTATO AND HOT DOG SALAD

6 medium potatoes, cooked, peeled and chilled; diced in
 ½-inch cubes
6 hot dogs, cut in ½-inch cubes
2 eggs
½ cup sugar
1 teaspoon powdered mustard
1 teaspoon flour
1 teaspoon cornstarch
¾ cup cider vinegar
1 tablespoon butter
1 teaspoon salt
1 cup canned, diced beets, drained

Mix the cubed potatoes and the cubed hot dogs together lightly. Set aside.

Beat the eggs until they are light and frothy. Make a
mixture of the sugar, mustard, flour and cornstarch. Add
this mixture gradually to the beaten eggs and continue to
beat until smooth. Continue beating, and add the vinegar
a little at a time. Beat for 1 minute longer. Place the mixture in the top of a double boiler over slowly boiling water
and cook until thickened. Add the butter and salt. Mix well
and remove from the heat. Allow the dressing to cool to
room temperature.

Pour the dressing over the potatoes and the hot dogs;
mix lightly. Add the diced beets and mix again lightly.
Chill in the refrigerator for 2 hours before serving. Serves
6 generously.

Chapter V

HOT DOG CASSEROLES

IF YOU HAVE casserole fans in your family, try making them with hot dogs. Due to their total meat content and delicate flavor, hot dogs in casseroles are wonderful.

Hot dog casseroles can be frozen with great success. Make two casseroles at the same time. Serve one and freeze the other for a future meal. This will save you precious time and money.

If you have hit the doldrums when it comes to making casseroles, try some of the delicious recipes in this chapter. If you have casserole recipes that contain meat, try substituting hot dogs the next time you make them, and you will be pleasantly surprised.

Protein packed hot dogs enhance the flavors of casseroles like nothing else!

HOT DOG CHILI PIE

8 hot dogs, diced in ½-inch cubes
1 cup taco-type corn chips, coarsely crushed
1 cup garlic-flavored potato chips, coarsely crushed
1 #300 can barbecue-style beans (1¾ cups)
1 10¼-ounce can chili con carne with kidney beans
⅓ cup warm water
¾ cup onion, diced in ¼-inch cubes
¾ cup mild Cheddar cheese, diced in ¼-inch cubes

Mix the hot dogs, corn chips and potato chips by tossing together lightly. Add the barbecue beans, the chili con carne, the warm water and the diced onion. Again, mix all the ingredients lightly.

Place in a 1½-quart buttered casserole. Press the mixture down lightly. Place in a 350° F. oven for 15 minutes.

Sprinkle the cubed cheese over the top and return to the oven for an additional 8 minutes or until the cheese has melted. Serve at once. Serves 6.

HOT DOG AND CHEESE BAKE

4 slices enriched white bread, lightly buttered
8 hot dogs
1 8-ounce package Velveeta cheese spread
2 eggs, slightly beaten
3 cups milk
½ teaspoon salt
¼ teaspoon pepper

Stack the buttered bread and then cut up into 1-inch squares. Cut the hot dogs into ¼-inch thick circles.

Place ¼ of the buttered bread squares and ¼ of the hot dog circles in the bottom of a buttered casserole. Slice the cheese and place ¼ of the slices over the hot dogs and the bread. Repeat, ending with a layer of cheese and hot dogs as the top.

Add the beaten eggs to the milk. Add the salt and pepper and mix well. Pour this mixture over the bread, cheese and hot dogs. Bake, uncovered, in a 350° F. oven for 1 hour. Serve piping hot. Serves 6.

HOT DOGS AND POTATOES IN ONE DISH

5 cups raw potatoes, sliced ¼ inch thick
10 hot dogs, sliced in ¼-inch circles
2 tablespoons melted butter
¾ cup onion, diced in ¼-inch cubes
½ teaspoon salt
½ teaspoon pepper
2 cups warm milk
1 cup shredded mild Cheddar cheese
8 slices of bacon, fried crisp and crumbled

Place a layer of half of the sliced potatoes and half of the hot dog circles over the bottom of a 2-quart casserole. Drizzle with half the butter and sprinkle on half the onions. Season with half the salt and pepper. Repeat again, using the remainder of the ingredients.

Pour the warm milk over the top of the casserole and bake in a 350° F. oven for 1 hour or until you can pierce the potatoes easily with a fork. Just before serving, sprinkle the cheese and crumbled bacon over the top and place under the broiler for 3 minutes or until the cheese has melted. Serves 6.

HOT DOG AND BEAN BAKE #1

1 1-pound can vegetarian baked beans, undrained
1 1-pound can butter beans, undrained
1 1-pound can kidney beans, undrained
1 tablespoon prepared yellow mustard
1 teaspoon Worcestershire sauce
½ cup onion, finely chopped
8 hot dogs, cut in 1-inch pieces
½ cup dark brown sugar
⅛ teaspoon ground cloves

Mix the three bean varieties together just as they come from the can. Add the mustard, Worcestershire sauce and onion. Mix very well, taking care not to mash the beans. Add the hot dog pieces and turn the mixture over several times so that they are evenly distributed throughout.

Place in a buttered casserole. Mix the brown sugar and cloves together until completely blended and then sprinkle this over the top of the beans.

Bake, uncovered, in a 350° F. oven for 35 minutes. Serve at once, piping hot. Serves 6 to 8.

HOT DOG AND BEAN BAKE #2

2 1-pound cans pork and beans
1 cup diced onion
¼ cup diced green pepper
1 teaspoon powdered mustard
1 tablespoon Worcestershire Sauce
6 hot dogs
6 slices bacon

Drain the beans and discard the pieces of pork. If left in, this makes the dish much too greasy. Add the onion, green pepper, mustard and Worcestershire sauce. Mix well, taking care not to mash the beans.

Place the beans in a shallow baking dish. Wrap each hot dog in one of the slices of bacon, fastening the bacon at each end with a toothpick. Place the bacon-wrapped hot dogs over the surface of the beans. Bake in a 350° F. oven for 35 minutes or until the bacon begins to get crisp. Place under the broiler for 5 minutes to thoroughly crisp the bacon before serving. Serves 6.

HOT DOG AND BEAN BAKE #3

8 hot dogs, sliced ⅛ inch thick
2 1-pound jars New England-style baked beans
¾ cup heavy whipping cream
1 3-inch diameter Bermuda onion, peeled and sliced ¼ inch
thick
½ cup diced bacon

Distribute the hot dog slices over the bottom of a shallow baking dish. Remove any pork pieces from the beans and discard, for this will make the dish too greasy.

Gently fold the whipping cream into the baked beans, taking care not to mash the beans. Pour this mixture over the wiener slices. Break the onion slices up into rings and place them over the beans. Sprinkle the diced bacon over the top of the onions and beans.

Place in a 350° F. oven for 1 hour or until the bacon pieces have become crisp and the top of the beans have developed a crust. Serve piping hot. Serves 6 to 8.

HOT DOG AND BEAN BAKE #4

2 10-ounce packages French-style frozen green beans,
thawed
8 hot dogs
8 10-inch slices bacon
1½ cups tomato sauce
1½ cups grated American cheese

Spread the thawed green beans over the bottom of a shallow baking dish. Wrap each hot dog in a slice of bacon; fasten with a toothpick. Place the hot dogs wrapped in bacon over the top of the green beans.

Pour the tomato sauce over the hot dogs and green beans. Sprinkle the American cheese over the top. Place in a 350° F. oven for 25 minutes or until the cheese is melted and bubbly. Serve at once, piping hot. Serves 4.

HOT DOG AND BEAN BAKE #5

1 #2 can yellow butter beans, drained
1 #2 can green baby lima beans, drained
1 #2 can cut green beans, drained
1 #2 can red kidney beans, drained
8 hot dogs, quartered
1 pound sliced American cheese with pimiento pieces

Place the butter beans, baby limas, green beans and kidney beans in a large bowl. Mix all well, taking care not to mash the beans.

In a buttered casserole, place half of the bean mix over the bottom. Smooth out, and place the hot dogs in a layer over the top. Cover the hot dogs with half of the slices of cheese.

Place the remainder of the beans over the hot dogs and cheese. Again smooth them out, and cover with the remaining pieces of cheese.

Place in a 350° F. oven for 35 minutes or until the cheese on top is melted and bubbly. Serve piping hot. Serves 8.

ORIENTAL HOT DOG CASSEROLE

1 #2 can French-style green beans, drained
1 1-pound can Chinese vegetables, drained
1 5-ounce can water chestnuts, drained and sliced ⅛ inch thick
½ cup chopped onion
6 hot dogs, cut in ¼-inch circles
1 10-ounce can cream of mushroom soup
1 cup shredded mild American cheese

Mix the green beans, Chinese vegetables, chestnuts, chopped onion and hot dogs together lightly. Add the cream of mushroom soup and mix again. Place in a buttered casserole. Press the mixture down with the back of a spoon and then sprinkle the cheese over the top.

Bake in a 350° F. oven for 1 hour or until the cheese is slightly browned and bubbly. Serve piping hot. Serves 6.

DOG AND YAM CASSEROLE

6 hot dogs
½ cup crunchy-style peanut butter
½ cup chopped Virginia-style peanuts
1 1½-pound can yams packed in syrup, drained
½ cup currant jelly
2 tablespoons water

Split the hot dogs lengthwise and spread the insides with the peanut butter. Arrange them over the bottom of a buttered baking dish. Sprinkle the chopped peanuts over the wieners.

Cut the yams in half; arrange the halves over the top of the hot dogs.

Mix the currant jelly and water together and pour a portion of the mixture over each of the yam halves. Place in a 375° F. oven for 25 minutes. Serves 6.

LAZY BONES CASSEROLE WITH HOT DOGS

6 medium-sized potatoes, scrubbed but not peeled
4 medium-sized onions, peeled
10 hot dogs
1 #300 can kidney beans, drained
3 strips of very lean bacon, diced in ¼-inch cubes
1 can condensed tomato soup
1 beef bouillon cube dissolved in ½ cup boiling water

Slice the unpeeled potatoes into uniform ¼-inch slices. Slice the onions into ¼-inch slices. Slice the hot dogs into ¼-inch circles.

In a lightly buttered 1½-quart casserole, place a layer of half of the sliced potatoes, a layer of half of the onions. Cover the surface with the hot dog slices. Layer the kidney beans over the hot dogs. Sprinkle half of the bacon cubes over the kidney beans and hot dogs. Repeat the layers, using up the remainder of the potatoes, kidney beans, hot dogs and bacon.

Mix the tomato soup with the boiling bouillon. Pour over the ingredients in the casserole. Cover and bake at 375° F. for 1 hour. Remove the cover and bake for an additional 30 minutes. Serve at once, piping hot. Serves 6.

RED AND GOLD HOT DOG CASSEROLE

12 hot dogs
¼ cup butter or margarine
¼ cup chopped onion
1 4-ounce can mushroom stems and pieces, drained
2 medium-sized boiled potatoes, diced in ½-inch cubes
1 3-inch dill pickle, sliced paper thin
½ cup pimiento-stuffed green olives, thinly sliced
½ teaspoon salt
¼ teaspoon pepper
½ teaspoon Accent
1 16-ounce carton dairy sour cream or sour half-and-half
2 hard-boiled eggs, diced in ¼-inch cubes
¾ cup grated American cheese
¼ cup chopped pimiento
3 medium-sized tomatoes, peeled and quartered

Cut the hot dogs up into ¼-inch circles and set aside. Melt the butter in a large skillet; add the chopped onion and saute until the onion is limp and transparent. Add the mushroom stems and pieces and continue to cook until they are slightly browned. Add the diced hot dogs and continue to cook until they begin to brown on the edges. Remove from heat.

Stir in the diced potatoes, the dill pickle slices, the olives, salt, pepper and Accent. Add the sour cream and turn the mixture over several times to mix well. Place in a 2-quart buttered casserole. Press the mixture down slightly and smooth the top. Sprinkle the diced eggs over all. Sprinkle with the grated cheese and the chopped pimiento. Place the 12 wedges of the tomato around the outer edge. Bake in a 350° F. oven for 30 minutes or until the cheese is melted and bubbly. Serves 6.

FRANK AND POTATO CASSEROLE

8 wieners, cut in thirds
6 medium-sized potatoes, peeled and quartered
2 tablespoons Heinz 57 Sauce
½ cup half-and-half cream
¼ cup melted butter
1 teaspoon baking powder
½ cup grated Cheddar cheese

Boil the potatoes in a small amount of salted water until they are tender enough to pierce with a fork. Drain and mash the potatoes well. Using a wire whisk or an electric mixer, beat in the Heinz 57 sauce and the cream. Add the melted butter and the baking powder and continue beating until the potatoes are very light and fluffy.

Place half of the wiener pieces over the bottom of a suitable buttered baking dish. Top the wiener pieces with the mashed potato mixture. Place the remainder of the wieners over the top of the mashed potatoes. Press them down into the potatoes. Sprinkle the grated Cheddar cheese over the top.

Bake in a 450° F. oven for 15 minutes or until the cheese has melted and become bubbly. Serve piping hot. Serves 6.

HOT DOG AND KRAUT CASSEROLE

2 1-pound cans sauerkraut
12 hot dogs
2 tablespoons caraway seed
6 whole peppercorns
12 juniper berries (optional but nice)
1 8-ounce can tomato sauce
1 cup dairy sour cream
1 tablespoon brown sugar

Rinse the sauerkraut under cold running water. Allow to drain well.

In the bottom of a 3-quart buttered casserole with a tightly fitting cover, place four of the hot dogs. Sprinkle a 1-inch layer of sauerkraut over the hot dogs. Sprinkle ⅓ of the caraway seed, 2 peppercorns and 4 juniper berries over the sauerkraut. Place four more hot dogs over the sauerkraut and follow with another layer of sauerkraut and spices. Repeat, ending with a layer of sauerkraut and spices.

Mix the tomato sauce, dairy sour cream and brown sugar together and pour over the casserole ingredients. Cover tightly and bake in a 350° F. oven for 45 minutes. Serve piping hot. Serves 6.

HOT DOG TAMALE PIE

2 tablespoons bacon fat
1 tablespoon chili powder
1 tablespoon flour
1 teaspoon onion salt
½ teaspoon garlic powder
½ cup water
10 hot dogs, diced in ¼-inch cubes
1 12-ounce can niblet corn, drained
½ cup sliced, pitted ripe olives
2 cups taco-type corn chips, coarsely crushed
½ cup grated American cheese

Melt the bacon fat in a saucepan; mix the flour and chili powder together and then stir into the melted fat. Add the onion salt and garlic powder. Cook over moderate heat until the mixture begins to bubble slightly. Add the water and continue to cook, stirring constantly, over moderate heat until thickened. Remove from heat and stir in the diced hot dogs, niblet corn and ripe olives. Mix all very well.

In the bottom of a buttered casserole, place ¾ cup of the crushed corn chips. Follow this with a layer of the hot dog mixture. Sprinkle with more corn chips and another layer of the hot dog mixture. Continue, alternating the layers, ending up with a layer of corn chips. Sprinkle the grated cheese over the top. Place in a 350° F. oven for 15 minutes or until the cheese has melted. Serve at once, piping hot. Serves 6.

WIENER RICE CASSEROLE

8 wieners, sliced ⅛ inch thick
1 cup instant rice, cooked according to package directions, or 2 cups fluffy cooked rice
2 cups milk
1½ cups cubed mild Cheddar cheese
2 eggs, beaten until lemon yellow
½ teaspoon salt
¼ teaspoon pepper
1 cup pimiento-stuffed olives, sliced ⅛ inch thick
¼ cup melted butter
½ cup fine breadcrumbs

Place the milk in the top of a double boiler over rapidly boiling water. Add the Cheddar cheese and continue to cook until the cheese has melted, stirring frequently to smoothly blend the mixture. Remove from heat and stir 3 tablespoons of the cheese sauce into the beaten eggs; then add the eggs to the cheese sauce and mix well. Add the cooked rice, salt and pepper. Mix very well.

In a suitable buttered baking dish, spread ¼ of the rice mixture over the bottom. Place ¼ of the wiener slices and ¼ of the olive slices over the rice. Add another layer of rice and another layer of wiener pieces and olive pieces. Continue, alternating layers, ending up with the rice mixture last.

Stir the bread crumbs into the melted butter; mix well. Sprinkle the buttered crumbs over the top of the layered rice mixture. Place in a 350° F. oven for 20 minutes or until the top is a golden brown. Serve at once, piping hot. Serves 6.

BAKED HOT DOG DELIGHT

2 #2 cans macaroni and cheese
1 1-ounce bag garlic-flavored potato chips
8 hot dogs, cut in ⅛-inch circles
1 tablespoon chopped green pepper
1 teaspoon Worcestershire sauce
1 tablespoon parsley, finely chopped
¼ cup butter
1 cup soft bread crumbs

Mix the macaroni and cheese and the hot dog circles together. Add the potato chips, green pepper, Worcestershire sauce and chopped parsley. Mix again and place in a suitable buttered casserole.

Melt the butter in a skillet and stir in the bread crumbs. Mix well so that all of the crumbs are evenly buttered. Spread the buttered crumbs over the surface of the casserole.

Place in a 350° F. oven for 25 minutes or until the crumbs are a rich golden brown. Serve at once, piping hot. Serves 6.

HOT DOG, CHEESE, OLIVE AND RICE BAKE

2 cups milk
1½ cups grated Cheddar cheese
2 eggs, slightly beaten
2 cups fluffy cooked rice
½ teaspoon salt
¼ teaspoon pepper
¼ cup parsley, finely chopped
1 cup pimiento-stuffed green olives, sliced ⅛ inch thick
12 hot dogs, halved lengthwise
½ cup buttered bread crumbs

Heat the milk in the top of a double boiler to just below the scalding point. Gradually add the grated cheese, stirring after each addition. Continue to cook until all of the cheese has melted. Stir three tablespoons of the hot mixture into the beaten eggs, and then add the beaten eggs to the cheese sauce. Mix well and continue to cook for a few minutes longer until thickened. Add the salt, pepper and parsley. Add the cooked rice, mix well and remove from heat.

Place 8 pieces of the sliced hot dogs, cut side down, over the bottom of a buttered 9x5x3-inch loaf pan or oblong baking dish. Place ⅓ of the olives over the hot dogs. Pour ⅓ of the cheese and rice mixture over the hot dogs and olives. Follow this with another layer of 8 hot dog pieces, olives and ⅓ of the rice and cheese mix. Repeat with the remainder of the hot dogs and olives, ending with the rice and cheese mixture as the last layer. Sprinkle the top with the buttered bread crumbs.

Bake in a 325° F. oven for 30 minutes or until the crumbs are a golden brown and the loaf is firm. Allow to cool for 5 minutes and then loosen the sides of the loaf with a sharp knife and turn out on a heated platter. Slice in 1½-inch thick slices. Garnish with additional sprigs of parsley for color. Serves 6.

POTATO SALAD CASSEROLE

4 cups cooked potatoes, peeled and diced in ½-inch cubes
2 tablespoons butter
½ cup onion, finely chopped
½ cup green pepper, finely chopped
½ cup water
¼ cup vinegar
1 tablespoon granulated sugar
2 teaspoons flour
½ teaspoon salt
¼ teaspoon pepper
2 tablespoons pimiento, finely diced
½ teaspoon celery seed
6 hot dogs, cut in half crosswise
6 10-inch strips lean bacon, cut in half crosswise
2 tablespoons parsley, finely chopped

Place the diced potatoes in a 2-quart buttered casserole.
Melt the butter in a small skillet and add the chopped onion and the green pepper. Saute over very low heat until the onion is transparent.

Place the water, vinegar, sugar, flour, salt, pepper, pimiento and celery seed in a bowl and mix well. Add to the onion and green pepper; continue to cook over low heat until the mixture has thickened and become somewhat transparent. Pour over the diced potatoes in the casserole.

Wrap each half of a hot dog in one of the half strips of bacon and fasten in place with a toothpick. Place the hot dog halves like the spokes of a wheel over the potato mixture. Place in a 375° F. oven for 20 minutes or until the bacon has become crisp and golden. Turn the hot dogs over once during the baking time to crisp the bacon evenly on both sides. Serves 6.

SURPRISE CASSEROLE

¼ pound dried chipped beef
1 cup boiling water
¼ cup butter or margarine
¼ cup chopped green pepper
1 cup chopped celery
¼ cup all-purpose flour
¼ teaspoon pepper
2 cups milk
1 12-ounce can vacuum-packed corn, drained
6 hot dogs, diced in ¼-inch cubes
1 cup lightly buttered bread crumbs

Using a kitchen shears, snip the beef up into ⅛-inch strips. Pour the boiling water over the strips of beef and allow to stand for 5 minutes.

Melt the butter in a 1½-quart saucepan. Drain the chipped beef well and discard the water. Add the drained beef to the melted butter. Add the green pepper and the celery. Saute over low heat until the celery is soft. Stir in the flour; add the pepper. Continue to cook over low heat until the mixture begins to bubble. Slowly add the milk, stirring constantly. Continue to cook over low heat until thickened. Remove from heat.

Mix the corn and hot dog cubes together. Place half the corn and hot dogs over the bottom of a buttered 1½-quart casserole; sprinkle with half the bread crumbs; follow this with half the chipped beef sauce mixture. Repeat with the remainder of the hot dogs and corn and the sauce mixture. Sprinkle the remaining ½ cup of crumbs over the top. Place in a 350° F. oven for 35 minutes or until the crumbs are a rich golden brown. Serves 6.

HOT DOG LAYERED CASSEROLE

1 12-ounce can niblet corn with pimiento
1 cup instant rice, as it comes from the package
½ teaspoon salt
¼ teaspoon pepper
2 8-ounce cans tomato sauce
¾ cup water
10 hot dogs, finely chopped
¾ cup onion, coarsely chopped
½ cup green pepper, diced in ¼-inch cubes
4 10-inch strips very lean bacon

Mix the niblet corn and the instant rice together. Sprinkle with the salt and pepper and place in the bottom of a buttered 1½-inch quart casserole which has a tightly fitting cover. Mix one of the cans of the tomato sauce with the water and pour this over the rice and corn.

Distribute the chopped hot dogs over the rice, corn and tomato sauce. Sprinkle the chopped onion over the hot dogs; sprinkle the green pepper over the onion. Pour the remaining can of tomato sauce over the top of the casserole. Do not disturb the layered arrangement. Lay the bacon strips over the top.

Bake, covered, in a 350° F. oven for 45 minutes. Then remove cover and reduce heat to 300° F. Bake for an additional 30 minutes or until the bacon strips are crisp and golden. Serve at once, piping hot. Serves 6.

Variation:

Add 1 4-ounce can of drained mushroom stems and pieces to the corn and rice mixture for a delightful flavor variation.

HOT DOG CASSEROLE WITH SOUR CREAM

8 hot dogs
4 tablespoons butter
3 tablespoons all-purpose flour
4 tablespoons milk
¼ teaspoon salt
¼ teaspoon pepper
¼ teaspoon paprika
1½ cups dairy sour cream
¾ cup mushroom stems and pieces, coarsely chopped
1 tablespoon onion, finely minced
½ cup buttered bread crumbs

Cut the hot dogs up into ¼-inch circles. Place the butter in a skillet over moderate heat and saute the hot dog circles until they just begin to turn a rich brown.

Place the flour and milk in the top of a double boiler and mix until smooth and blended. Add the salt, pepper, paprika and sour cream. Mix until well blended. Place over barely bubbling hot water and cook, stirring constantly, until the cream has thickened. Keep the heat very low or you will curdle the sour cream. Remove from heat and add the mushroom pieces and the minced onion. Mix well.

Place the sauteed hot dog circles and any butter you have left in the pan in the bottom of a suitable casserole. Pour the sour cream sauce over the hot dog pieces. Sprinkle the buttered bread crumbs over the top. Place in a 300° F. oven for 25 minutes or until the crumbs are a rich golden brown. Serve piping hot. Serves 6.

BEAN CURRY WITH FRANKS

3 packages frozen baby lima beans
2 beef bouillon cubes, dissolved in 1 cup boiling water
1 cup grated Cheddar cheese
1 cup diced onion
¼ cup melted butter
1½ cups seedless raisins
½ teaspoon salt
¼ teaspoon pepper
1 teaspoon curry powder
¼ teaspoon nutmeg
8 wieners, cut in thirds
6 lemon wedges

Place the lima beans in a large mixing bowl; break up any large frozen parts of the beans so that they can be evenly mixed with the other ingredients. Add the bouillon, Cheddar cheese and onion. Mix all well.

Add the melted butter, the raisins, salt, pepper, curry powder and nutmeg and again mix well.

Place half of the hot dogs over the bottom of a buttered casserole. Follow this with half of the bean mixture. Place the remainder of the hot dogs over the bean mixture. Top with the remainder of the bean mixture.

Place in a 350° F. oven for 25 minutes or until the raisins are puffy and the beans are tender. Invert the top of the casserole once during the baking period to prevent drying out. Serve at once, piping hot. Serve each portion with a wedge of lemon. Serves 6.

Chapter VI

HOT DOG MAIN DISHES

MEAT HAS ALWAYS been the most costly item of a meal. Perhaps that's why restaurants always price their meals by the type of meat cut they are serving.

Steaks, chops and roasts are costly no matter what the tide of the economic times is. Hot dogs, made of pure, lean meat contain the same proteins as steaks, chops and roasts. Isn't it good economy to substitute the economical, tasty hot dog for these more expensive cuts?

If you want good, nourishing meals for your family, plan them around hot dog main dishes. Hot dogs offer you triple savings.

First of all, they take less cooking time than any other meat on the market because they have been completely cooked before you buy them.

Secondly, hot dogs are loaded with pure economy when you compare their price to the other cuts of meat on your butcher's counter.

Thirdly, there is not a speck of waste to a hot dog. You are getting all meat—no bones, no thick fat, no inedible gristle. You are purchasing pure, waste-free meat for your precious food dollar. Hot dogs are great—especially when they form the main dish of your family's meal.

HOT DOG LOAF #1

8 ounces medium egg noodles, cooked until tender according to package directions
3 eggs, slightly beaten
½ cup milk
½ teaspoon salt
½ teaspoon Accent
1½ cups grated mild American cheese
¼ cup parsley, finely chopped
8 hot dogs

Mix the cooked noodles, eggs, milk, salt, Accent, grated cheese and parsley together well.

In a greased loaf pan, place one third of the mixture evenly over the bottom. Place 4 of the hot dogs the long way over the noodles. Place another third of the noodles over the hot dogs. Place the remaining 4 hot dogs lengthwise on top of this addition of noodles. The hot dogs should be placed so that when you slice the loaf, you will have circles of hot dog interspersed with noodles in each slice. Top with the remaining third of the noodles. Press the mixture down in the pan well so that there are no air pockets.

Bake in a 350° F. oven for 1 hour. Remove from the oven and allow to cool for 8 to 10 minutes, to set before slicing. Loosen from the loaf tin with a sharp knife and invert on platter. Slice in 2-inch thick slices with a very sharp knife. Serves 6.

HOT DOG LOAF #2

12 hot dogs
1 cup grated sharp Cheddar cheese
1 egg, beaten until lemon yellow
1 cup milk
1 teaspoon Worcestershire sauce
¾ cup fine cracker crumbs
1 teaspoon baking powder
2 tablespoons minced parsley
1 10-ounce package peas frozen in cream sauce

Chop the hot dogs until they are the consistency of coarse corn meal. Mix the chopped hot dogs and grated Cheddar together thoroughly. Add the beaten egg to the milk along with the Worcestershire sauce; mix well and then add to the hot dogs and cheese. Mix the finely crushed cracker crumbs and baking powder together; add to the hot dog mixture along with the parsley and stir well.

Place in a lightly buttered loaf pan. Bake in a 350° F. oven for 1 hour. Turn out on a heated platter.

Cook the peas as directed on the package. Cut the hot dog loaf into generous slices and pour the creamed peas over the top. Serves 6.

HOT DOG LOAF #3

10 hot dogs
1 cup canned tomatoes
1 cup canned peas, drained
1 cup canned diced carrots, drained
½ cup chopped cashew nuts
½ teaspoon salt
⅛ teaspoon pepper
½ teaspoon Accent
¼ cup minced onion
1 cup soft, white enriched bread crumbs
½ cup half-and-half cream
3 eggs, beaten until lemon yellow
1 tablespoon melted butter

Chop the hot dogs until they are the consistency of coarse corn meal. Mix the chopped hot dogs, tomatoes, peas, carrots, cashews, salt, Accent, pepper, onion and bread crumbs thoroughly.

Mix the cream and beaten eggs together and add to the mixture. Stir in the melted butter. Mix thoroughly and place in a lightly buttered loaf tin. Bake in a 350° F. oven for 1 hour or until the center is firm. Serve in 1½-inch slices. Serves 6 generously.

HOT DOG LOAF #4

12 hot dogs, very finely chopped
1½ pounds ground veal (double ground if possible)
1½ cups enriched white bread crumbs
1 teaspoon salt
¼ teaspoon pepper
½ cup onion, finely chopped
¼ cup parsley, finely chopped
1 canned pimiento, finely chopped (optional)
3 eggs, beaten until lemon yellow
1 cup milk
4 slices lean bacon

Mix the ground veal and the chopped hot dogs together. Add the bread crumbs, salt, pepper, onion, parsley, pimiento, beaten eggs and milk. Mix all very thoroughly and then knead much as you would bread. Form into an oblong loaf and place in a lightly greased baking pan. Lay the four strips of bacon over the top diagonally.

Bake in a 350° F. oven for 1½ hours. After removing the loaf from the oven, let it rest for 5 minutes before slicing. Serves 6 generously.

Note: This hot dog loaf is delicious when served cold. It is a good partner to potato salad, and it also makes delicious cold sandwiches.

TETRAZZINI HOT DOGS

½ cup butter or margarine
1 8-ounce can mushroom stems and pieces, drained
¼ cup flour
2 tablespoons instant chicken bouillon granules
2 cups boiling water
1 cup half-and-half cream
1 teaspoon Heinz 57 Sauce
½ teaspoon salt
¼ teaspoon pepper
12 hot dogs, sliced in ¼-inch circles
1 12-ounce package medium egg noodles, cooked according
  to package directions
¾ cup grated Parmesan cheese
½ teaspoon paprika

Melt the butter in a large skillet. Add the mushroom stems and pieces and saute until slightly browned. Push the mushrooms to one side and stir in the flour. Cook until bubbly. Mix the chicken bouillon granules in the boiling water and add to the flour, butter and mushrooms. Add the cream and the Heinz 57 sauce; cook over very low heat, stirring constantly, until the mixture has thickened and coats the spoon. Add the sliced hot dogs; mix until the hot dog pieces are coated with the thickened sauce. Set aside.

Place the cooked and drained noodles in a buttered baking dish and pour the sauce and the hot dogs over the top. Sprinkle the top of the dish with the grated cheese, then with the paprika. Bake in a 350° F. oven for 20 minutes or until the cheese turns a golden brown. Serves 6 generously.

SPAGHETTI HOT DOG DINNER

6 slices bacon, diced in ½-inch pieces
8 hot dogs, diced in ¼-inch cubes
¾ cup onion, diced in ¼-inch cubes
¼ cup green pepper, diced in ¼-inch cubes
1 #2 can tomatoes
1 pound Velveeta cheese
½ teaspoon salt
⅛ teaspoon pepper
1 4-ounce can mushroom stems and pieces, drained
8 ounces vermicelli spaghetti, cooked until tender according to package directions

Place the diced bacon in a large skillet and saute until it is a golden brown. Do not drain the bacon, for the drippings form part of the flavor of this dish. Add the cubed hot dogs to the bacon and saute until the edges begin to turn brown.

Add the onion, green pepper and tomatoes to the bacon and hot dogs. Bring to a boil and cook over moderate heat for 8 minutes or until the onion begins to become limp and transparent. Reduce the heat to simmer and add the Velveeta cheese, salt, pepper and mushroom stems and pieces.

Continue to cook over very low heat, stirring constantly, until the cheese has completely melted and is smoothly blended. Place the hot, cooked spaghetti in a deep serving dish and pour the cheese and hot dog mixture over the top. Serve at once. Serves 6 generously.

HOT DOGS AND BAKED BEANS DINNER

2   #303 cans baked beans in tomato sauce
½ teaspoon garlic salt
¼ teaspoon salt
⅛ teaspoon pepper
1 cup dairy sour cream
8 hot dogs, sliced in ½-inch circles
½ cup chopped parsley
¼ cup chopped onion

Drain away most of the juice from the canned beans. Place the beans in a 2-quart buttered baking dish along with the garlic salt, salt, pepper and ½ cup of the sour cream. Stir in the hot dog pieces, parsley and chopped onion.

Bake, uncovered, in a 375° F. oven for 20 minutes or until the beans are bubbling in the center. Serve with a dab of the remaining sour cream on each portion. Serves 6.

HOT DOGS WITH CRUNCHY NOODLES

1 12-ounce package enriched broad egg noodles
1 teaspoon salt
1 tablespoon cooking oil
6 hot dogs, cut in ⅛-inch slices
½ cup butter
1 tablespoon dehydrated parsley flakes

Set aside approximately 1 cup of the dry egg noodles just as they come from the package.

Bring 3 quarts of water to a rolling boil; add the salt and the remainder of the noodles. Cook over moderate heat until the noodles are tender and can be cut when pressed against the side of the kettle with a spoon or fork. Add the cooking oil to the cooked noodles, mixing well. (The addition of the oil to the cooking noodles prevents them from sticking together after they are drained.) Drain the noodles through a collander. Return the hot noodles to the pan in which they were cooked. Add the hot dogs and mix well with a light hand. Cover and set aside.

Place the cup of egg noodles between two dish towels and crush fairly well with a rolling pin. Melt the butter in a skillet and add the crushed (uncooked) egg noodles. Saute the egg noodle pieces until they turn a rich brown. Stir constantly to avoid burning. Remove the skillet from the heat immediately.

Mix the cooked noodles and hot dog slices with the browned noodle pieces and their butter. Add the dried parsley flakes and mix again lightly. Serve at once. Serves 6.

Note: This is a very popular dish with youngsters, because they enjoy the crunchiness of the "toasted" noodle pieces.

HOT DOG AND BEEF LOAF

1½ pounds ground chuck
½ pound hot dogs, either ground or chopped very finely
½ cup soft white enriched bread crumbs
2 eggs, beaten until lemon yellow
1 cup milk
1 teaspoon salt
1 teaspoon celery seed
¼ teaspoon pepper
1 teaspoon prepared yellow mustard
½ cup onion, finely grated

Mix the ground chuck and the ground hot dogs together thoroughly. Add the bread crumbs, eggs, milk, salt, celery seed, pepper, mustard and onion. Mix again until all is smoothly blended. Place the mixture in a lightly buttered 10x5x3-inch loaf pan. Press the mixture down to expel any air pockets.

Place in a 350° F. oven for 1 hour. Slice 1½ inches thick. Serves 6.

Note: This loaf is excellent if served cold for sandwiches. When using for sandwiches, chill thoroughly and slice ¼ inch thick. This loaf will make 18 sandwiches.

BAKED HOT DOG DINNER

12 hot dogs, cut crosswise into thirds
4 cups cooked, hot instant mashed potatoes, prepared according to package directions
2 tablespoons minced green onion
¼ cup chopped pimiento-stuffed green olives
2 tablespoons parsley, finely chopped
⅛ teaspoon pepper
¼ teaspoon paprika

Place the cut-up hot dogs in a lightly buttered shallow baking dish. Mix the hot mashed potatoes with the onion, green olives, parsley and pepper. Spread this mixture over the hot dogs. Arrange in decorative peaks.

Sprinkle the paprika over the mashed potatoes and bake in a 350° F. oven for 30 minutes or until the top has turned a golden brown. Serve piping hot. Serves 6.

HOT DOG JAMBALAYA

¼ cup bacon, diced in ¼-inch pieces
½ cup onion, diced in ¼-inch cubes
½ cup green pepper, diced in ¼-inch cubes
1 4-ounce can mushroom stems and pieces, drained
1 8-ounce can tomato sauce
1 cup instant rice, uncooked
12 hot dogs, cut up in ½-inch cubes
1 beef bouillon cube dissolved in 1 cup boiling water
½ teaspoon Worcestershire sauce
2 tablespoons parsley, finely chopped

Place the diced bacon in a 2-quart saucepan and saute until it begins to brown. Add the onion, green pepper and mushrooms, and saute until the onion begins to get limp and transparent.

Remove from heat and add the tomato sauce, instant rice, hot dog cubes, bouillon water and Worcestershire sauce. Mix all well and pour into a lightly buttered 1½-quart casserole.

Cover and place in a 350° F. oven for 40 minutes. Sprinkle the chopped parsley over the top and serve at once. Serves 6.

SKILLET HOT DOG DINNER

2 #300 cans of chili con carne (with kidney beans)
1 #2 can chick peas, drained
2 12-ounce cans vacuum packed corn niblets with pimiento, drained
10 hot dogs
1 cup grated American cheese

In a large skillet with a tightly fitting cover, combine the chili con carne, chick peas and the corn niblets. Mix all very well, cover and place over low heat for 10 minutes, stirring occasionally to prevent scorching.

Cut the hot dogs into 1-inch lengths and add to the chili mixture. Mix all gently, taking care not to mash the beans and chick peas. Press the mixture down and smooth it over with a rubber spatula.

Sprinkle the grated cheese over the top. Continue to cook, covered, for 5 minutes longer or until the cheese has melted and become soft. Serve piping hot. Serves 6.

SKILLET OF HOT DOGS, PINEAPPLE AND BEANS

8 hot dogs, cut into thirds
½ cup onion, coarsely chopped
¼ cup butter
2 1-pound cans pork and beans
1 #211 can (13½ ounces) pineapple chunks, drained
1 tablespoon Worcestershire sauce
1 teaspoon powdered mustard
¼ cup parsley, finely chopped

Place the hot dog pieces, onion and butter in a large heavy saucepan. Saute over low heat until the onion is glazed and transparent and the hot dogs begin to brown slightly.

Remove the pork pieces from the pork and beans and discard, as this added pork will make the dish too greasy. Add the beans to the onions and hot dogs; add the pineapple chunks and Worcestershire sauce. Sprinkle the powdered mustard over the surface. Mix all well, using a light touch so that the beans do not get mashed. Continue to cook over low heat for an additional 20 minutes or until all is heated through.

Remove from the heat and stir in the chopped parsley. Serve at once. Serves 6 generously.

HAWAIIAN BARBECUE WITH HOT DOGS

1 8-ounce can tomato sauce
¼ cup brown sugar, tightly packed
¼ cup cider vinegar
1 tablespoon minced onion
1 tablespoon celery seed
1 teaspoon powdered mustard
1 teaspoon chili powder
1 tablespoon Worcestershire sauce
12 hot dogs
1 14-ounce can pineapple spears, drained
1 #303 can Kadota figs, drained

In a 1-quart saucepan, mix the tomato sauce, brown sugar, cider vinegar, onion, celery seed, mustard, chili powder and Worcestershire sauce thoroughly. Place over moderate heat and bring to a rolling boil for 5 minutes. Stir frequently to prevent scorching.

Alternate the hot dogs with the pineapple spears in a lightly buttered shallow baking pan. Arrange the Kadota figs around the hot dogs and the pineapple spears. Pour the hot barbecue sauce over all.

Place in a 325° F. oven for 35 minutes. Turn the hot dogs and figs over several times during the baking period to distribute the flavors of the sauce. Serve piping hot with hot fluffy rice. Serves 6.

HOT DOGS WITH CHIVE POTATOES

12 to 15 small pink salad potatoes (approximately 2 pounds)
10 hot dogs, cut crosswise in 1-inch pieces
½ cup butter
3 tablespoons chives, finely chopped
2 tablespoons lemon juice
1 teaspoon grated lemon peel
¼ teaspoon salt
½ teaspoon Accent
⅛ teaspoon black pepper

Wash and scrub the potatoes well. Place in salted water to cover and boil until they are tender enough to pierce with a fork. Remove from the heat, drain and peel.

Add the hot dog pieces to the peeled hot potatoes and set aside.

Melt the butter in a large skillet; add the chopped chives, lemon juice and lemon peel. Stir well and then add the salt, Accent and black pepper. Place the hot dogs and the potatoes in the butter sauce and turn over lightly until all are coated with sauce.

Cook over very low heat for 10 minutes, turning gently from time to time. Serve at once, piping hot. Serves 6 generously.

Variations:

Substitute ¼ cup thinly-sliced scallions for the chives. Be sure to include a portion of the green.
If you cannot obtain small salad potatoes, use the larger variety and cut them into quarters after they are cooked and peeled.

71

HOT DOGS AND HASH-BROWNED POTATOES

8 hot dogs sliced in ¼-inch circles
6 medium-sized potatoes, scrubbed well but not peeled
4 tablespoons olive oil
4 tablespoons butter
2 cloves garlic, sliced 1/16 inch thick
½ teaspoon salt
¼ teaspoon pepper
3 scallions, cut into ⅛-inch slices (use a portion of the green too)
3 tablespoons parsley, finely chopped
1 tablespoon caraway seed

Boil the potatoes in their jackets until they are tender enough to pierce with a fork. Do not overcook or let them get too soft. Drain and peel. Slice the hot, peeled potatoes about ¼ inch thick; place in a mixing bowl, cover and set aside.

Place the olive oil, butter and garlic in an oven-proof skillet over moderate heat. Saute the garlic until it begins to turn brown. Using a slotted spoon, remove the garlic from the butter and olive oil. Add the potatoes to skillet and mix lightly with the olive oil and butter.

Add the sliced hot dogs, salt, pepper, scallion pieces, parsley and caraway seed. Mix all very well. Press down firmly in the skillet; smooth the top with a rubber spoon. Place the skillet over moderate heat until the bottom of the potatoes are a golden brown. Do not stir, but using a spatula, lift up a small portion to see if they are sufficiently browned.

Place the skillet about 6 inches away from the broiler heat and brown the top side. Loosen the potatoes and hot dogs with a spatula and turn out on to a heated platter. Serve at once, piping hot. Serves 6.

HOT DOG SPANISH RICE

6 slices lean bacon
8 hot dogs
¾ cup onion, coarsely chopped
¾ cup instant rice just as it comes from the package
1 cup boiling water
1 8-ounce can tomatoes (1 cup)
½ teaspoon salt
¼ teaspoon pepper

Cut the bacon into ¼-inch cubes and saute over low heat until slightly transparent but not crisp. Pour off any excess grease. Dice the hot dogs into ¼-inch cubes and add to the bacon along with the chopped onion. Continue to saute over low heat until the onion is limp and transparent. Remove from heat.

Mix the instant rice and the hot water; allow to stand for 5 minutes; then add the rice and water to the hot dog and onion mixture. Stir in the tomatoes, salt and pepper. Pour into a deep buttered baking dish. Cover and bake in a 350° F. oven for 20 minutes or until the rice has absorbed all of the liquid. Serve at once. Serves 6.

HOT DOG AUTUMN DISH

1 #2 can sweet potatoes, drained
4 medium-sized tart apples
12 hot dogs
½ cup dark brown sugar, tightly packed
¼ teaspoon cinnamon
¼ teaspoon grated lemon rind
1 teaspoon lemon juice
¼ cup melted butter
½ cup soft bread crumbs

Slice the sweet potatoes ½ inch thick. Peel, core and quarter the apples and then chop them coarsely. Cut the hot dogs crosswise diagonally into 1-inch pieces.

Place a layer of sweet potato slices over the bottom of a buttered 10x5x2-inch baking dish with a cover. Follow this with a layer of chopped apples and half of the diagonally-cut hot dogs.

Mix the brown sugar, cinnamon, lemon rind and lemon juice together. Sprinkle half of this mixture over the ingredients in the baking dish. Follow with the remainder of the sweet potato slices, apples and hot dogs. Again sprinkle with the remainder of the brown sugar mixture.

Mix the melted butter and the bread crumbs together and sprinkle this over the top of the other ingredients. Cover and place in a 350° F. oven for 1 hour. Remove the cover and bake for 5 minutes longer. Serves 6.

HOT DOG AND HAM LOAF

10 hot dogs, very finely chopped
¾ pound ground lean ham
1 cup dry bread crumbs
¼ cup onion, finely chopped
¼ cup celery, finely chopped
¼ teaspoon freshly ground pepper
1 egg, beaten until lemon yellow
¾ cup milk

Sauce:

⅓ cup grated horseradish, pressed dry
¼ cup mayonnaise
½ cup heavy whipping cream

Mix the chopped hot dogs, ground ham, bread crumbs, onion, celery and ground pepper together. Mix the egg and milk together and add to the hot dog mixture. Stir and mix all well.

Pour into a lightly buttered 9x5x3-inch loaf pan and bake in a 350° F. oven for 1 hour.

Whip the cream until it is stiff and stands in peaks. Fold in the mayonnaise and the horseradish.

Serve the hot ham loaf in 1½-inch slices topped with a portion of the sauce. Serves 6.

HOT DOGS AND ONION RINGS

8 hot dogs
1 8-ounce can tomato sauce
1 teaspoon powdered mustard
¼ teaspoon ground cloves
⅛ teaspoon sweet basil
1 teaspoon granulated sugar
1 tablespoon raw rice
1 10-ounce package frozen French fried onion rings

Quarter the hot dogs and place in a 1-quart saucepan along with the tomato sauce, mustard, cloves, basil, sugar and rice. Mix all well.

Cook over low heat, covered, for 20 minutes or until the rice grains are tender and the sauce has thickened to the consistency of catsup. Stir gently from time to time during this cooking period.

Place the French fried onion rings on an oven-proof serving platter. Place in a 375° F. oven for 10 minutes or until the rings are heated through and crisp.

Pour the hot dogs and their sauce over the heated onion rings and serve at once, piping hot. Serves 6.

HOT DOG NOODLE RING WITH SAUERKRAUT

1 #2½ can sauerkraut
1 cup tart baking apples, peeled and sliced
½ cup Rhine wine
½ teaspoon Accent
2 tablespoons dark brown sugar
¼ teaspoon pepper
6 juniper berries
1 16-ounce package medium-wide egg noodles, cooked until tender according to package directions; drained and slightly cooled
8 hot dogs, cut in ⅛-inch circles
¼ cup melted butter
¼ teaspoon pepper
½ teaspoon salt
¼ cup parsley, finely chopped
3 eggs, beaten until lemon yellow

Place the sauerkraut in a saucepan with a tightly fitting cover. Add the apple, Rhine wine, Accent, brown sugar, pepper and juniper berries. Mix well and bring to a rolling boil; turn heat down to low and simmer for 30 minutes, stirring occasionally.

In a large mixing bowl, mix the cooked noodles, hot dog slices, melted butter, salt, pepper and parsley. Fold in the beaten eggs. Place the mixture in a well-buttered 8½-cup ring mold. Press down so that there are no air pockets. Place in a 375° F. oven for 20 minutes or until the ring is firm in the center.

Remove the noodle ring by loosening the edges with a sharp knife; then invert on a platter. Spoon the hot sauerkraut mixture into the middle. Serve at once, piping hot. Makes 4 generous servings.

HOT DOGS, CHEESE AND POTATOES

12 hot dogs, diced in ¼-inch cubes
2 cups mild American cheese, diced in ¼-inch cubes
1 3-ounce can pimientos, drained and diced in ¼-inch cubes
3 cups cooked potatoes, diced in ½-inch cubes
¼ cup melted butter or margarine
¼ cup all-purpose flour
2 cups milk
½ teaspoon salt
¼ teaspoon pepper
2 tablespoons parsley, finely chopped

Place the diced hot dogs, cheese cubes, diced pimientos and diced potatoes in a large mixing bowl. Toss all together until uniformly mixed.

Melt the butter in the bottom of a 2-quart saucepan; stir in the flour and cook over low heat until bubbly. Add the milk. Stirring constantly, cook over low heat until the mixture has thickened. Add the salt, pepper and parsley to the sauce. Mix well.

Add the hot dog-potato mixture to the sauce and continue to cook over very low heat for 8 minutes or until warmed through, stirring frequently. Serve at once, piping hot. Serves 6.

Note: Do not be concerned if the cheese cubes do not melt thoroughly during the cooking time, for this is part of the deliciousness of this dish.

HOT DOGS AND AU GRATIN POTATOES

12 hot dogs
4 tablespoons butter
¼ cup green pepper, finely chopped
¼ cup canned pimiento, finely chopped
¼ cup onion, finely chopped
½ teaspoon salt
¼ teaspoon pepper
¼ teaspoon paprika
2 cups milk
2 cups grated American cheese
3 cups cooked potatoes, diced in ½-inch cubes

Cut the hot dogs in ¼-inch circles. Set aside. Melt the butter in a 1½-quart saucepan. Add the green pepper, pimiento, onion, salt, pepper, paprika and saute until the onion is limp and slightly transparent. Gradually add the milk, stirring constantly. Continue to cook over low heat. Add the grated cheese a little at a time; continue to cook until the cheese is melted. Remove from the heat.

Add the diced potatoes and mix well, taking care not to mash up the potato pieces. Place half of the sliced hot dogs in the bottom of a buttered casserole. Follow this with half of the potato mixture. Place the remainder of the hot dogs over the potatoes and again follow with the remainder of the potato mixture.

Place in a 350° F. oven for 30 minutes. Serve at once, piping hot. Serves 6.

HOT DOG-GHETTI DINNER

8 small onions, about 1 inch in diameter
1½ cups water
1 8-ounce can tomato sauce
1 #303 can tomatoes (2 cups)
1 cup spaghetti bends (small curved pieces of spaghetti)
1 package garlic-flavored salad dressing mix
½ cup sweet pickle relish, drained
8 hot dogs, cut in thirds

Peel the onions and place them in a saucepan with the water. Boil over moderate heat until the onions can be pierced with a fork. Drain, reserving the water in which they were boiled.

Place the reserved onion water in a 1½-quart saucepan along with the tomato sauce and tomatoes. Bring to a rolling boil, then add the spaghetti. Turn the heat back to simmer and cook for 25 minutes or until the spaghetti is tender, stirring occasionally.

Add the salad dressing mix, the pickle relish, whole onions and the hot dog pieces. Continue to cook over low heat for 10 minutes longer, stirring occasionally. Serve piping hot. Serves 6.

GONE TO THE DOGS HASH

2 tablespoons butter or margarine
¼ cup onion, thinly sliced
10 hot dogs, diced in ¼-inch cubes
1 tablespoon grated horseradish
1 tablespoon cider vinegar
1 teaspoon caraway seed
1½ cups cabbage, finely shredded (or leftover cole slaw which has been drained and pressed dry)
2 cups cooked potatoes, diced in ½-inch cubes

Melt the butter in a large skillet. Add the sliced onion and cook over low heat until the onion is limp and transparent. Add the hot dog cubes, horseradish, vinegar and caraway seed. Continue to cook over low heat for 8 minutes. Stir from time to time to mix the flavors.

Add the shredded cabbage, spreading over the top of the hot dogs; add the diced potatoes, spreading them over the top of the cabbage. Cover and continue to cook over very low heat for 5 minutes. Then completely turn the mixture over so that the potatoes are on the bottom of the pan. Continue to cook over very low heat for 5 additional minutes. Serve piping hot. Serves 6.

CREOLE HOT DOGS

3 tablespoons butter or margarine
¾ cup onion, coarsely chopped
½ cup celery, diagonally sliced ¼ inch thick
1 #2 can Italian tomatoes
1 8-ounce can tomato sauce
1 teaspoon chili powder
1 teaspoon brown sugar
½ teaspoon Accent
½ teaspoon salt
½ cup green pepper strips, 1x¼ inch thick
8 hot dogs, cut into fourths crosswise
4 cups cooked hot fluffy rice
2 tablespoons dehydrated parsley

Melt the butter in a large skillet; add the chopped onion and saute until the onion is limp and transparent. Add the celery. Continue to saute until the celery becomes transparent around the edges.

Add the tomatoes and the tomato sauce. Stir well; add the chili powder, brown sugar, Accent and salt. Continue to cook over low heat until it reaches a bubbling boil.

Add the green pepper strips and the pieces of hot dog. Turn the heat back to simmer and cook for 8 minutes longer or until the hot dog pieces are warmed through.

Stir the dehydrated parsley into the hot cooked rice. Spread the rice on a heated platter and pour the hot dog mixture over the rice. Serve at once, piping hot. Serves 6.

HOT POT KRAUT AND HOT DOGS

8 hot dogs, sliced in ¼-inch circles
1 #2½ can sauerkraut, undrained
1 cup water
1 #1 can small white onions, undrained
1 10-ounce package frozen carrots and peas
½ cup celery, diced in ¼-inch cubes
½ teaspoon caraway seed
½ teaspoon celery seed
¼ cup parsley, finely chopped
1 cup canned tomatoes
1 10-ounce package French-style frozen green beans
1 10-ounce can cream of celery soup
1 10-ounce can frozen potato soup

Place the hot dog slices, sauerkraut, water, onions and peas and carrots in a 2-quart saucepan over low heat. Add the celery, caraway seed, celery seed and parsley. Cook over low heat for 20 minutes. Do not cover; otherwise you will lose the bright colors of the vegetables. Turn the mixture over several times during cooking so that all is heated through and done evenly.

Add the tomatoes and the frozen green beans and continue to cook for 5 minutes longer or until the beans just begin to get tender. Stir in the celery soup and add the potato soup. Cook for an additional 8 minutes or until the potato soup is melted. Stir the mixture lightly so that the vegetables do not get crushed. Serve piping hot with saltine crackers or with crisp pieces of French bread. Serves 6.

HOT DOG AND NOODLE BAKE

1 6-ounce package medium egg noodles, cooked according to package directions
¼ cup butter or margarine
¼ cup chopped onion
¼ cup all-purpose flour
½ teaspoon powdered mustard
½ teaspoon salt
⅛ teaspoon pepper
1¼ cups milk
1 16-ounce package creamed cottage cheese
½ cup mushroom stems and pieces, drained
½ cup toasted sliced almonds
8 hot dogs, diced in ¼-inch cubes
1 cup grated American cheese

Drain and rinse the cooked noodles in cold water. Set aside to drain thoroughly. Melt the butter in a 2-quart saucepan and add the chopped onion. Cook the onion over moderate heat until it is transparent and limp. Mix the mustard, flour, salt and pepper together. Push the onions to one side of the saucepan and add the flour mixture to the melted butter. Stir well and cook over very low heat until it begins to bubble. Stir in the milk and continue to cook and stir over low heat until the mixture is smooth and thickened.

Stir in the drained noodles, the cottage cheese, the mushroom stems and pieces, the sliced almonds and the hot dog cubes. Mix all well with a light touch. Pour into a buttered 2½-quart baking dish.

Smooth the top of the mixture with the back of a spoon and then sprinkle the grated American cheese over the top. Bake in a 350° F. oven for 30 minutes or until the cheese is bubbly and lightly golden. Let stand for 5 minutes before serving for firmer portions. Serves 6.

HOT DOG 'N LIVER SAUSAGE LOAF

12 hot dogs
½ pound smoked liver sausage (at room temperature)
1½ cups soft enriched white bread crumbs
1 egg, beaten until lemon yellow
¾ cup half-and-half cream
½ teaspoon salt
½ teaspoon Accent
⅛ teaspoon pepper
4 strips bacon

Sauce (optional but good):

1 8-ounce can tomato sauce
½ cup celery, finely chopped
¼ cup green pepper, finely chopped
1 teaspoon brown sugar
1 drop Tabasco
1 teaspoon prepared yellow mustard
⅛ teaspoon ground cloves

Chop the hot dogs until they are the consistency of coarse corn meal. Peel and mash up the liver sausage; add to the chopped hot dogs along with the bread crumbs, beaten egg, cream, salt, Accent and pepper. Mix all thoroughly and pack into a lightly buttered loaf pan. Cut the bacon in half crosswise and place diagonally over the top.

Bake in a 350° F. oven for 45 minutes or until the bacon and the top of the loaf are a crisp golden brown. Slice in generous slices. Can be served hot or cold.

To make the sauce, combine all of the ingredients and simmer over low heat for 30 minutes or until thickened. Serve separately, allowing each person to spoon the sauce over the slice of loaf.

Serves 6.

DUCHESS POTATOES AND HOT DOGS

6 medium-sized potatoes, halved
¼ cup butter or margarine
½ cup hot half-and-half cream
½ teaspoon salt
½ teaspoon Accent
⅛ teaspoon pepper
2 egg yolks, beaten until lemon yellow
6 hot dogs
¼ cup melted butter (additional)
1 teaspoon paprika

Wash, peel and cook potato halves in water to cover for about 25 minutes or until tender enough to pierce with a fork. Drain and again place over the hot burner for 2 or 3 seconds to thoroughly dry them. Mash the potatoes thoroughly.

Using a whisk or electric mixer whip the butter into the potatoes. Gradually add the hot half-and-half cream and continue beating. Add the salt, Accent and pepper. Mix well. Beat two tablespoons of the hot potato mixture into the egg yolks and then beat the egg yolks into the mixture.

Slice the hot dogs lengthwise about half way through leaving a "hinge" at one side. Lay the hot dogs, cut side down, about 2 inches apart on a lightly buttered cooky sheet.

Using a pastry bag and the star-shaped tip, force the mashed potatoes over and around the hot dogs. For added color, leave each end of the hot dog peeking out from under the potatoes. Drizzle the melted butter over the mounds of potato. Sprinkle with paprika.

Place in a hot, 450° F. oven for 8 minutes or until golden brown. Remove from the cooky sheet with a spatula on to each plate. Serves 6.

Note: Leftover mashed potatoes can also be used for this dish. Place the leftover potatoes in a double boiler over barely boiling water until heated through. Whip again until fluffy and then add the egg yolks.

Packaged instant mashed potatoes can also be used in this recipe if you desire.

HOT DOGS IN PIQUANT MUSTARD SAUCE

12 hot dogs
1 cup granulated sugar
½ cup prepared horseradish mustard, Dusseldorf style
¼ cup vinegar
2 beef bouillon cubes dissolved in ½ cup water
2 egg yolks, beaten until lemon yellow
¼ cup butter
1 teaspoon flour

Cut the hot dogs in half lengthwise and arrange in the bottom of a lightly buttered shallow baking dish with a tightly fitting cover.

Mix the sugar, horseradish mustard, vinegar and bouillon in the top of a double boiler. Add the beaten eggs, butter and flour. Cook over rapidly boiling water, stirring constantly, until the mixture has thickened and coats the spoon.

Pour the mixture over the hot dogs in the baking dish. Cover and place in a 350° F. oven for 15 minutes or until the hot dogs are warmed through. Serve at once. Serves 6, allowing 4 hot dog halves per person.

HOT DOG AND ROASTED RICE CASSEROLE

8 hot dogs, sliced in ½-inch circles
1 cup raw long grain rice
1 foil package onion soup mix (1¼-ounce size)
2 cups boiling water or clear soup stock
1 tablespoon butter
1 tablespoon dehydrated parsley

Spread the rice over the bottom of an ungreased large shallow baking pan. Place in a 400° F. oven for 8 minutes or until the rice has toasted to a golden brown color. Shake the pan from time to time so that the rice is evenly browned. Remove from the oven and set aside.

In a 2-quart casserole with a tightly fitting cover, place the onion soup mix and the boiling water or soup stock. Stir to dissolve. Add the butter, parsley and the golden toasted rice. Add the hot dog slices. Mix all well, cover and bake at 350° F. for 30 minutes or until all of the liquid has been absorbed and the rice is light and fluffy. Serve at once, piping hot. Serves 6.

HOT DOG PICNIC LOAF

1 8-ounce package elbow macaroni, cooked according to package directions
1 teaspoon grated lemon rind
2 tablespoons lemon juice
1 teaspoon salt
¼ teaspoon pepper
2 teaspoons prepared yellow mustard

Sauce:

¼ cup all-purpose flour
2 cups milk
2 cups shredded Cheddar cheese
½ cup diced green pepper
¼ cup scallions, finely sliced (include some of the green please)
¼ cup canned pimiento, finely diced
¼ cup green olives, finely chopped
8 hot dogs
6 large lettuce leaves
3 tomatoes, quartered

Drain the macaroni and place in a 2-quart mixing bowl. Add the grated lemon, lemon juice, salt, pepper and mustard. Mix lightly. Set aside while you make the sauce.

Mix the flour and milk together in a saucepan. Place over low heat and cook, stirring constantly, until the mixture begins to coat the spoon. Add the cheese and continue to cook over low heat until the cheese is melted and the mixture just begins to bubble. Add the green pepper, scallion pieces, pimiento and olives. Mix well; add to the macaroni mixture and stir well.

Pour about two cups of the mixture into the bottom of a buttered 1½-quart loaf pan. Place four of the hot dogs lengthwise on the surface of the macaroni. Follow this with another cup of the macaroni mixture and four more hot dogs staggered in position from the first four hot dogs. Place the remainder of the macaroni mixture over the top. Press down with a spoon to force out any air pockets. Place in the refrigerator for at least six hours or overnight.

Place the lettuce leaves around the edge of a platter

and unmold the loaf on top of the lettuce leaves. Place six wedges of tomato on each side of the loaf. Serves 6 generously.

Variations:

Instead of leaving the hot dogs whole, chop them coarsely and mix them with the cheese sauce before combining with the macaroni.

Substitute ½ cup pitted ripe olives for the green olives; chop them coarsely; eliminate the pimiento.

SHOESTRING HOT DOG DISH

12 hot dogs
¼ cup chopped onion
¼ cup butter or margarine
1 tablespoon brown sugar
1 teaspoon prepared yellow mustard
⅛ teaspoon pepper
2 beef bouillon cubes dissolved in ½ cup boiling water
¼ cup cider vinegar
1 tablespoon Worcestershire sauce
1 drop Tabasco
½ cup tomato sauce

Slice the hot dogs into quarters the long way; then cut the quarters in half crosswise. Each hot dog should yield 8 pieces. Set aside.

Melt the butter in the bottom of a 1-quart kettle with a tightly fitting cover. Add the onions to the melted butter and saute until they are limp and slightly transparent. Add the sugar, mustard, pepper, bouillon water, vinegar, Worcestershire sauce, Tabasco and tomato sauce. Mix all well and bring to a boil.

Add the hot dogs to the boiling sauce and mix lightly so that all the hot dog pieces are coated. Turn the heat back to simmer, cover and cook for 20 minutes, turning the hot dogs occasionally so that the flavors are evenly blended. Serve piping hot. Serves 6.

Note: This dish is excellent with hot fluffy rice.

Chapter VII

HOT DOG SANDWICHES SUPREME

THAT SUCCULENT MORSEL, a hot dog in a soft bun with mustard and relish, is not to be looked down upon. However, there are many other ways to make a hot dog sandwich.

Since the hot dog is thoroughly cooked when purchased, it lends itself to chopping, grinding and slicing. Due to the hot dog's delicate flavor, it bends over backwards to get along with other good ingredients. Using hot dogs in sandwiches is a natural.

When you mention a hot dog sandwich, most people conjure up a vision of that wiener in a bun; that's only natural because this is how they were introduced to the U. S. A.

Down with mere wieners in a bun! Revolutionize your sandwich-making by introducing your family to some of the delicious combinations in this chapter.

HOT DOG CANOES

12 slices soft enriched white bread, crusts removed
½ cup melted butter
6 slices process American cheese 3x3x⅛ inch thick
2 tablespoons Dusseldorf-style mustard
12 hot dogs

Brush one side of each slice of bread with the melted butter. Cut the slices of cheese into 4 equal strips and place a strip on the unbuttered side of the bread. Brush the bread and cheese with the mustard. Place a hot dog on top of the cheese and bring up two opposite corners of the bread to meet on top of the hot dog. Fasten the bread in place with a toothpick.

Place on a cooky sheet in a 350° F. oven for 8 to 10 minutes or until the bread has toasted to a crisp brown on the outside. Serve at once, piping hot. Serves 6, allowing two hot dog canoes per person.

HOT DOG SANDWICH

8 hot dogs, halved lengthwise
4 tablespoons Kitchen Bouquet
½ cup melted butter
1 clove garlic, minced
8 slices enriched white bread
1 cup grated American Cheese

Brush the hot dogs on their cut side with the Kitchen Bouquet and set aside.

Place the minced garlic in the melted butter over very low heat for about 5 minutes to allow the flavors to unite. Brush each piece of bread with some of the garlic butter.

Place the pieces of buttered bread on a cooky sheet. Sprinkle each piece with a portion of the grated cheese. Place two halves of the flavored hot dogs, cut side up, on top of the cheese.

Place in a 400° F. oven for 8 minutes or until the cheese has melted and the hot dogs are just beginning to get brown. Serve at once. Serves 8, allowing 1 open sandwich per person.

HOT DOG OPEN FACE SANDWICHES

8 hot dogs
1 3-ounce package cream cheese, at room temperature
1 teaspoon horseradish-flavored mustard
2 tablespoons half-and-half cream or milk
1 tablespoon parsley, finely chopped
8 hamburger buns
1 teaspoon paprika

Chop the hot dogs until they are the consistency of hamburger. Mix the chopped hot dogs, cream cheese, mustard, cream and parsley together well.

Split the hamburger buns in half, and spread each half with the mixture. Sprinkle each with a portion of the paprika.

Place on a cooky sheet, spread side up, and broil about 6 inches from the heat for 8 minutes or until the sandwiches begin to brown. Serve at once. Serves 8.

DOG-BEANWICHES

1 10-ounce can bean soup with bacon
6 hot dogs, diced in ¼-inch cubes
3 slices American cheese with pimiento, 3x3x⅛ inch thick
4 scallions, sliced 1/16 inch thick (include a little of the green)
½ cup drained ripe olives, thinly sliced
6 hamburger buns, halved
¼ cup melted butter

Place the bean soup in a mixing bowl just as it comes from the can. Add the cubed hot dogs. Cut the cheese up into ¼-inch cubes and add to the beans and the hot dogs. Add the sliced scallions and the sliced ripe olives. Scoop out the soft center of the top of each hamburger bun, leaving about a ½-inch wall. Crumble up the soft bread center and add it to the bean mixture. Stir until all is well blended.

Brush the bottom and the scooped out half of each bun with the melted butter; place, open sides up, under the broiler for a few seconds or until they have just turned a crisp golden brown.

Fill the top half cavity of each bun with the hot dog-bean filling. Place on the bottom half of the bun and wrap tightly in a square of aluminum foil. Place the foil-wrapped buns on a cooky sheet and bake at 350° F. for 10 minutes. Serves 6, allowing 1 sandwich per person.

DOWN EAST BAKED BEAN AND HOT DOG RAREBIT

1 cup baked beans; these can be leftovers or drained pork and beans
8 hot dogs, diced in ¼-inch cubes
1 cup milk
1 tablespoon butter
1 cup grated mild American cheese
1 egg, slightly beaten
¼ teaspoon salt
¼ teaspoon prepared yellow mustard
¼ teaspoon Worcestershire sauce
3 4-inch diameter English muffins, cut in half and toasted or 6 thick slices enriched white bread, toasted

Mash the baked beans until they are fairly smooth. Mix with the diced hot dogs and set aside.

Heat the milk in the top of the double boiler to just below the scalding point; add the butter and gradually stir in the grated cheese. Continue to cook and stir until smooth. Take 2 tablespoons of the cheese mixture and stir it into the beaten egg; then add the beaten egg to the cheese mixture. Stir well. Add the salt, mustard and Worcestershire sauce. Add the mashed beans and the hot dogs. Mix all well, and continue to cook for 5 minutes longer or until all is warmed through.

Serve in generous portions over the toasted English muffin halves or over toasted bread. Serves 6.

HOT DOG RIB LINERS

10 hot dogs
2 cups chopped, roasted, lean pork
⅔ cup grated sharp American cheese
¼ cup grated onion
⅓ cup mayonnaise
12 hamburger buns, halved

Chop the hot dogs until they are the consistency of coarse corn meal. Add the chopped roast pork, cheese and grated onion. Add the mayonnaise and mix all thoroughly.

Scoop out a portion of the dough from the top half of the hamburger buns, leaving about ½-inch wall. Fill this cavity with a portion of the hot dog mixture. Cover with the bottom half. Wrap each bun in aluminum foil.

Place the foil-wrapped sandwiches in a 375° F. oven for 15 minutes. Serve piping hot. Serves 6, allowing 2 sandwiches per person.

Variations:

Substitute ¼ cup French dressing for the mayonnaise for a different flavor.

Use a mixture of chopped roast pork and chopped roast veal instead of all pork.

Place a thin slice of tomato on top of the sandwich filling before wrapping in foil and placing in the oven.

Add ¼ cup chopped tart apple to the filling for a different flavor.

TACO HOT DOGS

12 hot dogs
¾ cup taco-type corn chips
2 cups grated American cheese
2 tablespoons grated onion
1 teaspoon Worcestershire sauce
½ cup mashed avocado pear
1 cup lettuce, finely shredded
12 hot dog buns

Cut the hot dogs open the long way, leaving a "hinge" at one side. Set aside. Crush the corn chips until they are very fine. Add ½ cup of the grated cheese. Reserve the rest. Add the grated onion, Worcestershire sauce and the avocado pear. Mix all very well. Stuff the center of each hot dog with the mixture.

Cut the hot dog buns open also leaving a "hinge" at one side. Place them, open side up, on a cooky sheet. Sprinkle each bun with a bit of the shredded lettuce. Place a filled hot dog on top of the lettuce in each bun and sprinkle a portion of the grated cheese over all.

Broil about 8 inches away from the heat until the cheese just begins to melt. Serve at once. Serves 6, allowing two per person.

HOT DOG POPS

12 hot dogs
1½ cups sifted flour
2 teaspoons baking powder
¼ teaspoon salt
1 cup milk
1 egg, beaten until lemon yellow
1 tablespoon melted butter
12 wooden skewers such as the butcher uses for mock chicken legs
Deep vegetable oil for frying

Sift the flour, baking powder and salt together twice. Mix the milk and egg together and stir into the flour until you have a smooth batter. Add the melted butter gradually and mix well.

Dry the hot dogs with paper toweling so that they contain absolutely no moisture. Stick a skewer into one end of the hot dog so that it reaches about halfway up into the inside. Using the skewer as a handle, dip each hot dog into the batter, allowing the batter to come up about ½ inch on to the skewer. Drop the batter covered hot dogs into 350° F. vegetable oil and fry until the batter turns a golden brown.

Remove the hot dogs to paper toweling and allow to drain slightly. Serve piping hot. Serves 6, allowing 2 hot dogs per person.

Note: These batter covered hot dogs can be made in advance and reheated in the oven on a pan with a rack. These hot dogs are very popular for children's parties. If very tiny tots are involved, omit using skewers in the hot dogs, for they can prove dangerous. The hot dogs can be dipped and fried without the sticks.

GLAZED HOT DOGS

12 hot dogs
1 cup apple butter
1 teaspoon grated lemon rind
1 teaspoon grated orange rind
12 hot dog buns
½ cup melted butter
½ cup chopped walnut meats

Place the hot dogs side by side in a shallow baking dish.

Mix the apple butter thoroughly with the lemon and orange rind. Pour the apple butter over and around the hot dogs. Place in a 325° F. oven for 25 minutes or until the apple butter is bubbly. Turn the hot dogs over once during this baking time.

Split the hot dog buns open just half way through. Place the buns, open side up, on a broiler rack. Brush the interior of each bun with melted butter; sprinkle the interior of the buns with a portion of the nut meats. Broil about 6 inches away from the heat for 5 minutes or until lightly toasted. Serve the glazed hot dogs in the toasted buns. Spoon a little of the apple butter left in the pan over each hot dog. Serves 6, allowing two per person.

SUPER SUPER HOT DOGS

½ pound ground chuck
¼ cup onion, finely chopped
2 tablespoons green pepper, finely chopped
1 clove garlic, finely crushed
½ teaspoon salt
¼ teaspoon seasoned pepper (obtainable in spice section of supermarkets)
½ teaspoon chili powder
½ teaspoon powdered mustard
2 tablespoons brown sugar
juice of ½ lemon
1 cup tomato sauce
8 hot dogs
8 hot dog buns

Place the ground chuck in a skillet over low heat. Saute until the meat loses its reddish color and begins to brown slightly. Add the onion and continue to saute until the edges of the onion begin to get transparent. Add the green pepper, garlic, salt, seasoned pepper, chili powder, mustard, brown sugar, lemon juice and tomato sauce. Cook over low heat for 25 minutes, stirring frequently.

Place three tablespoons of the beef-barbecue mixture in each hot dog bun; place the hot dog on top of the barbecue sauce; wrap each hot dog sandwich in aluminum foil, sealing tightly. Place the hot dog sandwiches on a cooky sheet in a 375° F. oven for 20 minutes. Serve at once, piping hot. Serves 8, allowing one hot dog per person.

HOT DOG CHEESE RAREBIT

4 English muffins, halved and lightly toasted
8 hot dogs
¼ cup soft butter
1 cup grated Cheddar cheese
¼ teaspoon salt
⅛ teaspoon pepper
¼ teaspoon paprika
2 tablespoons brandy
¾ cup mushroom stems and pieces, finely chopped
1 egg

Cut the hot dogs in half lengthwise and place the 2 halves, cut side down, on each toasted muffin half.

Mix the soft butter and cheese together until you have a soft spreadable mixture. Add the salt, pepper, paprika, brandy and the chopped mushrooms. Mix well, and then add the egg and beat until all is well blended.

Spread a portion of the mixture over and around the hot dog halves. Place the muffin halves on a cooky sheet in a 350° F. oven for 20 minutes or until the tops are bubbly and slightly browned.

Serve at once. Serves 4, allowing 2 muffin halves per person.

Variations:

Use ¾-inch thick slices of enriched white bread in place of each muffin half.
Use halves of hard rolls in place of the muffins.
Substitute American cheese for the Cheddar cheese.
Substitute Swiss cheese for the Cheddar cheese.

HOT DOG SURPRISE

10 hot dogs
5 hard-boiled eggs, chilled and peeled
½ cup sweet pickle relish, pressed dry
1 cup grated sharp Cheddar cheese
½ cup onion, finely chopped
½ cup peanuts, finely chopped
¼ cup mayonnaise
1 tablespoon prepared mustard
12 hot dog buns, halved

Chop the hot dogs and the hard-boiled eggs together until they are the same consistency as the pickle relish. Add the pickle relish, the grated cheese, chopped onion, chopped peanuts, mayonnaise and prepared mustard. Mix all thoroughly.

Scoop out about half the dough from the top half of the hot dog buns, leaving a ½-inch wall. Fill this cavity with the hot dog mixture. Cover with the bottom half. Wrap each filled bun in a square of aluminum foil. Place the foil-wrapped buns on a cooky sheet in a 300° F. oven for 20 minutes. Serve piping hot. Serves 6, allowing 2 sandwiches per person.

SWISS 'N WIENER SANDWICHES

4 hot dogs
4 hard-boiled eggs, cooled and peeled
½ cup cabbage, very finely chopped
¾ cup Swiss Cheese, diced in ¼-inch cubes
3 tablespoons ripe olives, finely chopped
2 tablespoons parsley, finely chopped
½ cup dairy sour cream
¼ cup mayonnaise
16 slices rye bread, lightly buttered

Chop the hot dogs and the hard-boiled eggs until they are about the size of small peas. Add the finely-chopped cabbage, the diced Swiss cheese, the ripe olives and the parsley.

Mix the sour cream and the mayonnaise together and add to the hot dog mixture. Mix all very well.

Spread the mixture on 8 of the slices of buttered rye bread; top with the remaining 8 slices. Cut each sandwich diagonally into thirds. Garnish with ripe or green olives. Makes 8 generous sandwiches.

Variations:

Substitute mild American cheese for the Swiss cheese.
Substitute mild Cheddar cheese for the Swiss cheese.
Use whole wheat bread in place of the rye bread.
Add 1 tablespoon of finely grated onion for more zip.
Add 2 tablespoons of chili sauce and reduce the mayonnaise to 3 tablespoons.

SURPRISE SANDWICHES

4 hard-boiled eggs, peeled and coarsely chopped
1 cup American cheese, diced in ¼-inch cubes
½ cup mayonnaise
2 tablespoons green pepper, finely chopped
2 tablespoons onion, finely chopped
2 tablespoons parsley, finely chopped
2 tablespoons sweet pickles, finely chopped, or drained pickle relish
8 hot dogs, finely chopped
8 hamburger buns

Mix the chopped eggs, cheese, mayonnaise, green pepper, onion, parsley, sweet pickle and hot dogs together well. Place a heaping spoonful of the mixture in the center of each hamburger bun. Wrap tightly in aluminum foil and place on a cooky sheet.

Bake in a 350° F. oven for 30 minutes. Serve at once. Serves 8.

HOT DOG ROUND-UP SANDWICHES

8 hot dogs
8 round hard rolls, 3 inches in diameter
1 #2½ can sauerkraut
1 teaspoon celery seed
½ cup catsup
2 tablespoons capers, finely chopped
1 teaspoon caraway seed
½ cup soft butter
1 tablespoon grated horseradish
1 teaspoon prepared yellow mustard

Drain the sauerkraut and press dry. Chop with a chopping blade until quite fine. Add the celery seed, catsup, capers and caraway seed. Place in the top of double boiler over slowly boiling water for 20 minutes to unite all of the flavors.

Mix the butter, horseradish and mustard together thoroughly. Cut off the top quarter of the hard rolls. Dig out the soft dough in the center forming a cup-like indentation in the roll. Spread the interior of each roll with some of the flavored butter. Place on a cooky sheet in a 450° F. oven for 5 minutes or until a delicate golden brown.

Make 12 slashes along one side of each hot dog. Make the slashes about halfway through the hot dogs. Drop the hot dogs into boiling water. Bring up to a full boil, cover and remove from the heat. Set aside for 5 minutes.

Remove the hot dogs from the water, and form into circles, slashed side out. Place the hot dog circles inside the buttered rolls. Fill the center of each hot dog circle with some of the sauerkraut mixture. Return to the 450° F. oven for 5 minutes longer. Serve at once. Serves 8.

FRENCH-TOASTED SURPRISES

8 hot dogs
1 cup pitted ripe olives
½ cup diced green pepper
½ cup diced sweet onion
1 clove garlic
¾ cup mayonnaise
½ cup catsup
½ teaspoon Accent
½ teaspoon salt
¼ teaspoon pepper
½ teaspoon paprika
12 slices enriched white bread
2 eggs, beaten until lemon yellow
½ cup half-and-half cream
½ cup sesame seed
½ cup soft butter

Chop the hot dogs, pitted olives, green pepper, onion and garlic until they are the consistency of hamburger. Add the mayonnaise, catsup, Accent, salt, pepper and paprika. Mix all very well. Spread the mixture on six slices of the bread. Top with the remaining six slices and press together firmly.

Mix the beaten eggs and the cream together. Dip each sandwich in it, and then sprinkle lightly with the sesame seed. Saute in the butter in a large skillet over moderate heat. Saute the sandwiches as you would French toast until they are a golden brown on each side. Serve piping hot with pickle chips or sweet-and-sour pickles as a garnish. Serves 6.

HOT DOGWICHES

8 hot dogs
½ cup chopped onion
¾ cup Velveeta cheese, diced in ¼-inch cubes
½ cup fresh tomato, diced in ¼-inch cubes
½ cup mayonnaise
1 teaspoon prepared yellow mustard
1 tablespoon dehydrated parsley
8 hamburger buns, sliced in half

Chop the hot dogs fairly fine; add the chopped onion, Velveeta, diced tomato and mix all well.

Mix the mayonnaise, mustard and parsley together; add to the hot dog mixture. Mix all well.

Scoop out the soft dough in the top part of the hamburger buns. Fill this cavity with a portion of the hot dog mixture. Place on top of the bun bottom. Wrap each bun in a square of aluminum foil.

Place the foil-wrapped sandwiches on a cooky sheet in a 350° F. oven for 30 minutes. Serve at once, piping hot. Serves 8, allowing 1 sandwich per person.

HOT DOG PASTIES

8 hot dogs
1 tablespoon vegetable shortening
¼ cup raw carrots, finely chopped
2 tablespoons onion, finely chopped
1 medium-sized tomato, peeled and chopped
1 medium-sized cooked potato, coarsely chopped
¼ teaspoon pepper
2 cups biscuit mix
⅓ cup milk

Chop the hot dogs until they are the consistency of peas. Melt the shortening in a skillet and saute the carrots and onion until lightly browned. Add the chopped hot dogs and saute until they are warmed through and just lightly browned. Add the chopped tomato, potato, salt and pepper. Mix well; cook for a few seconds and then remove from heat and set aside.

Mix the biscuit mix and the milk together until smooth. Turn out on a floured board or pastry cloth and knead until you have a smooth dough. Roll out to ¼ inch thickness. Cut into 4-inch circles. Place a spoonful of the hot dog mixture on one half of the circle. Wet the outer edge of the circle with a little cold water and fold over to form a half circle over the filling. Press the dampened edge of the circle tightly so that the filling is completely sealed inside.

Place the half circles on a lightly buttered cooky sheet and bake in a 350° F. oven for 15 minutes or until a delicate golden brown. Serve at once. Serves 6.

OVERNIGHT HOT DOG SANDWICHES

Here is a dish that your family will not tire of. It takes a little time, for it has to marinate in the refrigerator overnight or at least 8 hours. However, the reward in unique flavors is well worth it.

2 cups grated mild American cheese
8 hot dogs, finely chopped
1 3-ounce package cream cheese, at room temperature
18 slices square sandwich-style enriched white bread, crusts removed
4 eggs, beaten until lemon yellow
2½ cups milk
⅛ teaspoon salt
⅛ teaspoon pepper

Sandwich topping:

1 tablespoon butter
½ cup chopped onion
1 10-ounce can cream of mushroom soup
1 cup half-and-half cream
3 hard-boiled eggs, peeled and coarsely chopped
1 tablespoon parsley, finely chopped

Mix the grated American cheese, chopped hot dogs and the cream cheese together until it is of spreading consistency.

Spread this mixture on one side of twelve of the pieces of bread. The remaining six are reserved for the top. Place six of the spread slices, spread side up, on the bottom of a suitable baking dish. Follow this by placing the remaining six slices of spread bread on top, again with the spread side up. Top with the remaining six slices of unspread bread. You will end up with a three-layer sandwich. Press down on each sandwich slightly so that the layers are firmly adhered.

Mix the eggs, milk, salt and pepper together well. Pour this over the three-layer sandwiches. Cover with aluminum foil and place in the refrigerator overnight.

The following day, remove the foil cover and place in a 325° F. oven for 45 minutes or until firm and just slightly browned.

For the topping, melt the butter in a saucepan; add the

onion and saute until it is slightly transparent. Add the mushroom soup and cream and stir well. Continue to cook over low heat for 5 minutes or until warmed through. Add the chopped eggs and the parsley; cook for 3 minutes longer. Stir from time to time to prevent sticking.

Using a broad spatula, remove each sandwich from the baking dish to individual serving dishes. Top each baked sandwich with generous spoonfuls of the sauce. Serve piping hot. Serves 6.

HOT DOG SLOPPY JOES

8 hot dogs
½ cup onion, finely chopped
2 tablespoons butter
1 cup celery, finely chopped
2 8-ounce cans tomato sauce
2 tablespoons cornstarch
½ cup chili sauce
½ teaspoon salt
¼ teaspoon pepper
8 hamburger buns

Slice the hot dogs up into ⅛-inch circles. Set aside. Place the butter in a large skillet and add the onion. Saute until the onion is transparent; add the celery and continue to cook until the largest pieces of celery are tender and soft.

Stir the cornstarch into the tomato sauce until it is completely dissolved. Add to the onion and celery mixture. Stir in the chili sauce, salt, pepper and hot dog pieces.

Cook over very low heat for 25 minutes or until thickened. Stir frequently to prevent sticking.

Serve by placing large spoonfuls between heated hamburger buns. Serves 8.

SAUERKRAUT AND WIENER SANDWICHES

1#2 can sauerkraut, drained and pressed dry
1 cup raw carrot, finely grated
¼ cup chopped green pepper
¼ cup chopped sweet red pepper
1 cup mayonnaise
1 teaspoon celery seed
1 teaspoon poppy seed
8 hot dogs, cut in half lengthwise
8 slices enriched white bread

Chop the sauerkraut with a chopping knife until it is as fine as the grated carrots. Combine the sauerkraut, grated carrot, green pepper, red pepper, mayonnaise, celery seed and poppy seed; mix all thoroughly.

Spread each piece of bread with a portion of the mixture. Place the hot dog halves, skin side up, on top of the kraut mixture. Place the slices of bread on a cooky sheet, broil about 6 inches from heat for 8 minutes or until the hot dogs begin to brown slightly. Serve at once. Serves 8, allowing 1 sandwich for each person.

Note: The relish mixture can also be used in hot dog buns with separately grilled or boiled hot dogs.

HOT DOG TRIOS

4 slices rye bread
4 slices white bread
4 slices whole wheat bread
½ cup soft butter
2 slices Swiss cheese (sandwich size)
2 slices Brick cheese (sandwich size)
2 slices American cheese (sandwich size)
6 hot dogs
3 eggs, beaten until lemon yellow
1 teaspoon Worcestershire sauce
2 drops Tabasco
1½ cups milk
1½ cups grated Cheddar cheese
6 slices tomato, ½ inch thick, approximately 3 inches in diameter

Lightly butter each slice of bread on one side. Place two

slices each, buttered side up, of the three kinds of bread over the bottom of a lightly buttered baking pan. Place a slice of Swiss cheese on the rye bread, a slice of Brick cheese on the whole wheat, a slice of American on the white bread.

Cut each hot dog into 3 slices lengthwise and place on top of the cheese. Place the corresponding slice of buttered bread on top of each hot dog.

Mix the eggs, Worcestershire sauce, Tabasco and milk together and pour over and around the sandwiches. Sprinkle the grated Cheddar over the top. Place in a 350° F. oven for 20 minutes or until the cheese topping has melted and become slightly puffed up. Place a slice of tomato on top of each sandwich and return to the oven for 8 minutes longer. Serve by using a broad spatula to transfer each sandwich to the plate; spoon some of the pan sauce over each. Serves 6.

HOT DOGS SUPREME

12 hot dogs
4 tablespoons onion juice, either fresh or bottled
6 pieces American cheese, 3x3x⅛ inch thick
12 10-inch strips bacon
12 hot dog buns

Slit the hot dogs on one side, but do not cut all the way through. Leave a "hinge" at one side. Brush the inside of each hot dog with the onion juice.

Cut the cheese into ½-inch strips and place two of the strips inside each slit hot dog. Fasten a strip of bacon to one end of the hot dog with a toothpick and spiral it around the cheese-filled hot dog barber-pole style. Fasten the bacon on the other end of the hot dog with a toothpick. Brush the bacon with some of the onion juice.

Place in the broiler or on the grill about 6 inches away from the heat. Broil, turning the hot dogs with tongs, until the bacon is crisp and golden on all sides.

Place the wrapped hot dogs in a bun, remove the toothpicks and serve. Serves 6, allowing two hot dogs per person.

Chapter VIII

HOT DOGS AND VEGETABLES

HOT DOGS and vegetables go together like ham and eggs. In this day of frozen vegetables, beautifully canned vegetables and fresh crisp produce, the average homemaker has a choice that would have made her grandmother's head whirl.

Our daily diets and our tables probably boast more good vegetables than granny's did even on Thanksgiving day. If you want to send your vegetable platter from the "no-thank-you" class to the "may-I-have-seconds?" class, try cooking them with hot dogs.

Because hot dogs are delicately spiced, they boost vegetable flavors but still firmly retain their own identity. Vitamins, minerals and protein all in one dish is what you will offer your family when you combine vegetables with hot dogs. If you have never joined a hot dog with a vegetable, start today—you will please your family if you do.

HOT DOG SUCCOTASH

8 hot dogs
1 #2 can lima beans, drained
1 #2 can creamed corn
4 tablespoons butter
½ cup half-and-half cream
½ teaspoon salt
¼ teaspoon pepper
1 tablespoon dehydrated parsley

Cut the hot dogs into 1-inch lengths. Place in the top of the double boiler. Add the drained lima beans, creamed corn, butter, cream, salt, pepper and parsley.

Mix all thoroughly, cover, and cook over slowly boiling water for 20 minutes. Serve piping hot. Serves 6.

HOT DOGS AND GREEN BEANS

2 pounds green beans
6 slices lean bacon
6 hot dogs
¼ cup onion, finely chopped
1 tablespoon vinegar

Wash and remove the stems and ends from the green beans. Cut each bean in half or in quarters diagonally, depending upon their size. Cover with cold water and cook over moderate heat until the beans are tender but not mushy. Drain and set aside in the kettle in which they were cooked.

Dice the bacon in ¼-inch cubes and place in a skillet over moderate heat. Saute the bacon until it just begins to get crisp and golden. Dice the hot dogs in ½-inch cubes and add them to the bacon. Saute until the hot dog pieces just begin to brown.

Remove from the heat and stir in the onion and the vinegar. Pour this mixture over the beans and mix well. Return to the heat for 5 minutes or until the beans are piping hot. Serves 6.

ZUCCHINI AND HOT DOG SAUTE

6 hot dogs, sliced in ⅛-inch thick circles
2 pounds small zucchini, about 1-inch in diameter
⅓ cup olive oil
2 tablespoons parsley, finely chopped
1 clove garlic, finely chopped
¼ teaspoon oregano
½ teaspoon salt
¼ teaspoon black pepper

Wash the zucchini thoroughly and remove the stem ends. Slice, without peeling, into ⅛-inch thick slices. Place the olive oil in a large skillet over moderate heat. When hot, add the zucchini and hot dog circles. Saute over moderate heat until the zucchini has browned, turning frequently.

Reduce the heat to simmer and add the parsley, garlic, oregano, salt and pepper. Stir lightly to distribute the flavors. Simmer for 5 minutes longer. Serves 6.

HOT DOGS AND CABBAGE WITH SOUR CREAM DRESSING

6 cups cabbage, coarsely shredded
8 hot dogs
1 tablespoon all-purpose flour
¼ teaspoon powdered mustard
½ teaspoon salt
⅛ teaspoon pepper
2 eggs, beaten until lemon yellow
½ cup dairy sour cream
3 tablespoons cider vinegar
2 drops Tabasco

Place the shredded cabbage in a suitable saucepan with water to cover over moderate heat. Bring to a rolling boil and cook for 5 minutes or until the thick portions of the cabbage can barely be pierced with a fork. The cabbage should remain fairly crisp.

Slice the hot dogs lengthwise into quarters and then slice them in half crosswise, ending up with 8 strips each. Drop the hot dog pieces into the boiling cabbage and turn several times so that all of the hot dog pieces become heated through. Remove from the heat and set aside.

Mix the flour, mustard, salt and pepper together in the top of a double boiler. Add the eggs, sour cream, vinegar and Tabasco and mix well. Cook over slowly boiling water until thickened. Stir constantly to keep the mixture smooth and creamy.

Drain the hot dogs and the cabbage well. Place in a heated serving dish and pour the thickened dressing over all. Serves 6.

HOT DOG AND SPINACH BAKE

10 hot dogs
2 10-ounce packages of frozen chopped spinach, cooked according to package directions and drained
1½ cups grated American cheese
1 teaspoon garlic salt
2 tablespoons dehydrated onion
¾ cup instant rice, just as it comes from the package
2 eggs, beaten until lemon yellow
2 cups milk

Cut the hot dogs into ½-inch thick circles and place over the bottom of a buttered 10x8x2-inch deep baking dish.

Place the drained, cooked, chopped spinach into a large mixing bowl. Add the cheese, garlic salt, onion and rice. Mix all well. Add the beaten eggs to the milk and mix well. Add the eggs and milk to the spinach and rice mixture. Mix thoroughly and pour over the sliced hot dogs.

Place in a 325° F. oven for 40 minutes or until the center is firm to the touch. Serve by scooping up a portion of the hot dogs at the bottom and inverting over the rice and spinach custard. Serves 6.

GREEN AND YELLOW BEAN AND HOT DOG MEDLEY

1 #2 can green beans, undrained
1 #2 can yellow wax beans, undrained
8 hot dogs
¾ teaspoon powdered mustard
1 teaspoon flour
½ teaspoon salt
⅛ teaspoon pepper
2 egg yolks, beaten until lemon yellow
1 tablespoon butter or margarine
1 cup scalded milk
2 tablespoons fresh lemon juice

Place both cans of beans and their liquid in a 1½-quart saucepan over moderate heat. Cut the hot dogs into quarters the long way and then cut them in half crosswise. After the beans have reached the boiling point, turn off the heat and add the hot dog strips. Set aside while preparing the sauce.

In a 1-quart saucepan, mix the mustard, flour, salt and pepper together. Add the beaten egg yolks and blend until smooth. Gradually add the scalded milk; add the butter and mix well. Place over very low heat and cook, stirring constantly, until the mixture has thickened. Rapidly stir in the lemon juice. Turn off the heat.

Drain the bean and hot dog mixture and place on a heated serving dish. Pour the sauce over all. Serve at once. Serves 6.

TOMATOES WITH HOT DOG STUFFING #1

6 ripe but firm tomatoes, about 3 inches in diameter
½ teaspoon salt
½ teaspoon seasoned pepper
1 10-ounce package frozen tiny peas
½ cup onion, finely diced
1 cup water
6 hot dogs, diced in ¼-inch cubes
6 tablespoons grated Parmesan cheese

Cut off a ½-inch slice from the blossom end of the tomatoes and discard. Scoop out the inside of the tomatoes, leaving a firm wall about ½ inch thick. Sprinkle the salt and seasoned pepper inside the tomatoes and set aside inverted upside down so that they drain.

Discard the seedy sections from the scooped-out tomatoes. Cut the remainder into ¼-inch cubes.

Place the frozen peas, the onion and the water in a saucepan over moderate heat. Bring to a rolling boil for about 3 minutes. Drain and discard the water.

Add the cubed tomato pieces to the peas and onions. Add the diced hot dogs and mix all well. Place a portion of the mixture in each drained tomato shell. Place in a baking dish, and then put 1 tablespoon of the Parmesan cheese on top of each filled tomato.

Bake in a 350° F. oven for 5 to 8 minutes; they should just be heated through, but not baked until mushy or shriveled. Serve at once. Serves 6.

TOMATOES WITH HOT DOG STUFFING #2

6 large ripe firm tomatoes
1 teaspoon Accent
4 tablespoons butter
1 tablespoon onion, finely chopped
6 hot dogs, finely chopped
½ cup bread crumbs
½ teaspoon salt
¼ teaspoon celery salt
¼ teaspoon pepper
2 eggs, beaten until lemon yellow
2 additional tablespoons butter

Cut the tops from the tomatoes and discard. Scoop out the inside pulp, leaving about ½-inch wall. Reserve the pulp until later. Invert the tomatoes on paper toweling and allow the excess juice to drain away. Let drain for ½ hour. Then turn the open side up and sprinkle the cavity with a portion of the Accent.

Melt the butter in a skillet over moderate heat. Add the onions and saute until limp and transparent. Chop the tomato pulp until it is fairly fine and add to the onion and butter; cook over low heat for 5 minutes or until the pulp is slightly thickened.

Add the hot dogs, bread crumbs, salt, celery salt and pepper. Remove from the heat and mix all well. Add the beaten eggs and mix well again.

Stuff each tomato with the mixture and place in a lightly buttered baking dish. Place a portion of the butter on top of each stuffed tomato. Bake in a 350° F. oven for 35 minutes. Serves 6.

HOT DOG TOMATO SCRAMBLE

4 slices bacon, diced in ¼-inch pieces
6 hot dogs, diced in ¼-inch pieces
3 medium-sized fresh tomatoes; firm but ripe
½ teaspoon salt
¼ teaspoon pepper
6 eggs, beaten until frothy

Saute the bacon in a suitable skillet over moderate heat until it just begins to turn a golden brown. Add the diced hot dogs and continue to saute until the hot dogs begin to get brown on the edges. Remove the bacon and hot dogs from the skillet with a slotted spoon and set them aside on absorbent toweling in a warm oven.

Peel the tomatoes, cut them up into eighths and place them in the remaining bacon fat over low heat. Sprinkle the tomatoes with the salt and pepper. Cover, and cook for 8 minutes or until the tomatoes are bubbling and slightly thickened. Stir from time to time.

Add the beaten eggs to the tomatoes and continue to cook over low heat. Stir slowly until the eggs are light and fluffy and completely cooked. Place on a heated platter. Sprinkle the top with the diced hot dog and bacon pieces. Serve at once. Serves 6.

GREEN BEANS AND HOT DOGS IN MUSTARD SAUCE

2 10-ounce packages frozen French-style green beans
10 hot dogs, cut crosswise in 1-inch pieces
1 cup half-and-half cream
2 tablespoons granulated sugar
2 tablespoons powdered mustard
1 tablespoon cornstarch
½ teaspoon salt
1 egg yolk, beaten until lemon yellow
2 tablespoons cider vinegar

Cook the frozen French-style beans according to the package directions. Do not drain, but turn off the heat and add the hot dog pieces so that they are warmed through in the hot bean water.

Place ¾ cup of cream in the top of a double boiler over slowly boiling water. Cook until the cream is scalded. In the remaining ¼ cup of cream, stir in the sugar, mustard, cornstarch and salt. Mix well and then slowly add to the scalded milk. Turn the heat to very low, and continue to cook, stirring constantly, for 8 minutes or until the mixture thickens. Stir about 2 tablespoons of the thickened sauce into the beaten yolk and then add to the sauce. Continue to cook over simmering water for an additional 3 minutes, stirring constantly. The sauce should be fairly thick. Remove from the heat and add the vinegar.

Drain the beans and hot dogs and place them on a heated platter. Pour the sauce over the hot dogs and beans and serve. Serves 6.

HOT DOG STUFFED ONIONS

6 large onions, about 3 inches in diameter
6 hot dogs
1 cup soft white enriched breadcrumbs
1 teaspoon ground sage
⅛ teaspoon pepper
¼ cup melted butter
½ cup grated American cheese

Peel the onions and place in a 2-quart kettle with enough water to cover. Boil until just tender enough to pierce with a fork. Drain and cool. Using a teaspoon, scoop out the centers of the onion, leaving about a ½-inch wall.

Place the scooped-out onion centers and the hot dogs in a chopping bowl. Chop until they are the consistency of coarse corn meal. Add ½ cup of the bread crumbs, the sage and pepper. Fill each onion cavity with the mixture, mounding the mixture up on each onion. Place the onions in a shallow baking dish. Brush the tops with a portion of the melted butter. Cover the dish with aluminum foil and place in a 350° F. oven for 20 minutes.

At the end of this baking time, mix the remainder of the bread crumbs, melted butter and grated cheese together and sprinkle it over and around the onions. Return to the 350° F. oven for an additional 10 minutes or until the cheese and crumbs have turned a rich golden brown. Serve piping hot. Serves 6.

ENDIVE CHARLOTTE WITH HOT DOGS

1 medium-sized head endive
6 slices bacon
2 tablespoons butter
4 hot dogs
4 eggs, well beaten
¼ cup granulated sugar
½ teaspoon salt
⅛ teaspoon pepper
3 tablespoons cider vinegar

Wash the endive thoroughly, discarding any tough outside leaves. Using a kitchen shears, snip the endive up into 3-inch long pieces. Set aside.

Dice the bacon in ½-inch pieces; place in a large skillet over moderate heat. Saute the bacon until it is just barely crisp. Dice the hot dogs in ¼-inch cubes and add to the sauteed bacon along with the butter. Continue to cook until the butter has melted. Remove from the heat and allow to cool slightly.

Add the well-beaten eggs gradually to the bacon mixture. Stir constantly. Add the sugar, salt, pepper and vinegar. Mix all well. Return the mixture to very low heat and add the snipped endive. Cook over very low heat, stirring and turning over constantly, until the endive has wilted and is coated with the mixture. Serve at once. Serves 6.

BEANS AND HOT DOGS, GREEK STYLE

1 pound dried white beans, soaked overnight in water to cover
½ cup olive or peanut oil
4 cloves garlic, very finely chopped
1½ cups onion, sliced ¼ inch thick
3 tablespoons dehydrated parsley
1 bay leaf, broken into bits
¼ teaspoon marjoram
¼ teaspoon savory
¼ teaspoon thyme
1 #2½ can tomatoes
1 teaspoon Accent
½ teaspoon salt
¼ teaspoon pepper
8 hot dogs, cut in 2-inch lengths

Drain the water from the soaked beans and discard. Rinse the drained beans under cold running water for a few seconds and then drain again. Set aside.

Heat the oil in the bottom of a 2-quart kettle. Add the garlic and onions and saute until the onions are limp and transparent. Add the bay leaf, marjoram, savory, thyme and tomatoes. Cook over moderate heat, stirring frequently, until the sauce becomes as thick as catsup. Add the drained beans, Accent, salt and pepper. Mix well. Add enough water to cover the beans. Cover and cook at simmer for 1 hour and 30 minutes. Remove the cover, add the hot dog pieces, mix well, and continue to cook, uncovered, for 30 minutes longer. The sauce around the beans and the hot dogs should be thick and a rich tomato color. Serve piping hot. Serves 6.

HOT DOGS, RED CABBAGE AND CHESTNUTS

½ pound chestnuts
1 head red cabbage (about 2 pounds)
1 teaspoon salt
½ cup brown sugar
1 tablespoon caraway seed
¼ cup butter
8 hot dogs, cut in 1-inch pieces
⅓ cup cider vinegar

Using a very sharp knife, cut a slit in the side of each chestnut. Place the gashed chestnuts in a saucepan with enough water to cover. Bring to a boil and cook for 20 minutes. Remove from the heat, but do not drain. Remove two or three chestnuts from the water at a time, when they are cool enough to handle, and remove the brown outer shell and the brown membrane covering. Slice each peeled chestnut into ⅛-inch slices. Set aside.

Remove any wilted outer leaves from the cabbage and discard. Rinse under running water. Cut the head of cabbage into quarters and remove the hard center core. Cut the cabbage up into ½-inch slices.

Bring enough water to cover the cabbage to a rolling boil. Add the salt, brown sugar and caraway seed. Add the shredded cabbage. Cook for 10 minutes or until the thickest parts of the cabbage can be pierced with a fork. Remove from the heat and drain; discarding the water in which the cabbage was boiled. Set the cabbage aside.

Melt the butter in a skillet; add the hot dog pieces and saute until they just begin to brown. Add the sliced chestnuts and the cider vinegar. Mix well, and pour over the boiled cabbage. Toss lightly so that all is evenly mixed. Serve at once. Serves 6.

BARBECUED HOT DOGS AND ONIONS

8 hot dogs
1 8-ounce can tomato sauce
½ teaspoon powdered mustard
¼ teaspoon ground cloves
⅛ teaspoon sweet basil
1 teaspoon granulated sugar
1 10-ounce package frozen French fried onion rings

Cut the hot dogs diagonally into thirds and place in a 1-quart saucepan along with the tomato sauce, mustard, cloves, basil and sugar. Cook over low heat, uncovered, for 20 minutes or until the sauce has thickened to the consistency of catsup, stirring gently from time to time.

Place the French fried onion rings on an oven-proof serving platter. Place in a 375° F. oven for 8 to 10 minutes or until the rings are heated through and crisp.

Pour the hot dogs and their sauce over the heated onion rings and serve at once. Serves 6.

ASPARAGUS AND HOT DOGS #1

6 slices enriched white bread
¼ cup soft butter
6 hot dogs
1 #2 can asparagus spears, either green or white, undrained
4 egg whites
¼ teaspoon cream of tartar
¼ cup mayonnaise
½ teaspoon salt
½ teaspoon prepared mustard
1 tablespoon fresh lemon juice
1 teaspoon Accent

Butter one side of the bread and toast it under the broiler until a golden brown. Butter the other side and toast it until golden brown. Slice each hot dog the long way and lay the two halves diagonally across the toasted bread. Set aside.

Place the asparagus and its juice in a saucepan, taking care not to break off any of the tender tips. Bring to a rolling boil for 5 minutes and then drain. Place two of the hot asparagus spears diagonally on each side of the hot dogs. Do not worry if the spears extend over the edge of the toast.

Beat the egg whites until they are frothy and bubbly. Add the cream of tartar and continue to beat until they stand in stiff peaks. Mix the mayonnaise, salt, mustard, lemon juice and Accent together well. Fold this mixture into the stiff egg whites. Using a rubber spoon, spread this mixture over the hot dogs and asparagus. Heap it up slightly in the center. Broil about 6 inches from heat until a delicate golden brown. Serve at once. Serves 6.

ASPARAGUS AND HOT DOGS #2

1 #2 can white asparagus spears, drained
8 hot dogs
4 hard-boiled eggs, chilled and peeled
1 cup grated American cheese
2 tablespoons butter
2 tablespoons flour
1 cup milk
½ teaspoon salt
¼ teaspoon pepper
1 cup coarse cracker crumbs

Alternate the asparagus spears and the hot dogs in a baking dish. Slice the hard-boiled eggs and place egg slices over the asparagus and hot dogs. Sprinkle the grated cheese over the top of the eggs.

Melt the butter in a saucepan over low heat. Stir in the flour and continue to cook until it begins to bubble. Gradually add the milk. Continue to cook over low heat, stirring constantly, until the mixture is thickened and coats the spoon. Add the salt and pepper, mix, and pour over the grated cheese.

Sprinkle the coarse cracker crumbs over the top of the dish and place in a 350° F. oven for 20 minutes or until the cracker crumbs are brown. Serve immediately. Serves 6.

KIDNEY BEANS WITH HOT DOGS

2 cups dry kidney beans, soaked overnight in water to cover
4 cups water (additional)
¾ cup dark corn syrup
¼ cup cider vinegar
1 teaspoon salt
¼ teaspoon pepper
½ cup green pepper, diced in ¼-inch cubes
½ cup celery heart, cut in ⅛-inch slices
8 hot dogs, cut in 1-inch pieces

Drain the kidney beans, discarding the water in which they were soaked. Bring the four cups of water to a rolling boil in a suitable saucepan with a tightly fitting cover. Add the soaked beans to the boiling water gradually so that the water does not stop boiling. Cover tightly, and cook over moderate heat for 1 hour or until the beans are tender enough to pierce with a fork. Keep the beans covered with water during the cooking; if some of the water evaporates away, add more.

Do not drain the beans, but add the corn syrup, vinegar, salt and pepper right to the beans and the water in which they were boiled. Mix thoroughly, and cook over moderate heat, uncovered, for an additional 30 minutes or until the juice has thickened. Stir frequently and gently. Add the green pepper, celery and hot dog pieces and cook over low heat for an additional 8 minutes. Serve immediately. Serves 6.

CHICK PEAS AND HOT DOGS

1 pound dried chick peas, soaked overnight in water to
   cover
½ teaspoon salt
1 medium-sized bay leaf
¼ cup peanut oil
2 cloves garlic, finely minced
1½ cups onion, finely chopped
½ teaspoon chili powder
8 hot dogs, cut crosswise in 1-inch pieces
1 tablespoon wine vinegar
1 8-ounce can tomato sauce

Add more water to the chick peas while they are soaking
if necessary. Often, depending upon the degree of dryness,
they will expand and absorb much of the water, leaving
the top layers uncovered. After soaking, drain and discard
the water in which they were soaked. Rinse under cold
running water for several minutes. Place in a 2-quart kettle
with water to cover, add the salt and the bay leaf. Place
over moderate heat and cook for 1½ hours or until the
peas can be pierced with a fork. Drain, reserving 2 cups
of the water in which they were boiled.

Heat the peanut oil in a skillet; add the garlic and onions.
Saute them until the onion becomes slightly browned. Add
the chili powder. Mix well and then add the hot dog pieces.
Saute for 5 minutes longer or until the hot dogs begin to
turn slightly brown. Mix the wine vinegar and tomato sauce
and add to the onion-hot dog mixture. Stir well and remove from the heat.

Place the drained chick peas in a suitable casserole; add
the reserved 2 cups of water and the hot dog mixture.
Stir well and cover; place in a 350° F. oven for 40 minutes.
Uncover and bake for 15 minutes longer. Serve piping
hot. Serves 6.

HOT DOGS AND PINTO BEANS

1 pound dried pinto beans, soaked overnight in water to cover
6 strips lean bacon, cut in ¼-inch pieces
¾ cup onion, coarsely chopped
1 clove garlic, finely chopped
½ cup warm water (additional)
1 teaspoon salt
¼ teaspoon pepper
½ teaspoon powdered mustard
1 teaspoon pulverized sage
2 teaspoons brown sugar
8 hot dogs, cut in 1-inch pieces

Drain the beans and discard the water in which they were soaked. Rinse the beans under cold running water for several seconds, and then drain again. Place the beans in a 2-quart kettle and cover with cold water. Place over moderate heat and bring to a boil; turn the heat back to low and continue to cook the beans at low while you prepare the other ingredients.

Place the bacon in a skillet over moderate heat and saute until the bacon is crisp and golden. Using a slotted spoon, remove the pieces of bacon and add them to the boiling beans.

In the remaining bacon fat, saute the onions and garlic until they are limp and transparent and just beginning to brown. Drain off the excess fat and discard. Add the sauteed onions and garlic to the boiling beans.

To the ½ cup of warm water, add the salt, pepper, mustard, sage and brown sugar. Mix well and add to the boiling beans. Stir the beans so that all of the flavors are distributed, cover, and continue to cook at low heat for 1 hour and 45 minutes, stirring occasionally.

At the end of this cooking period, add the hot dog pieces and continue to cook, without covering, for an additional 15 minutes. Serve piping hot. Serves 6.

SAUERKRAUT AND WIENERS

2 #2 cans sauerkraut
6 slices very lean bacon, cut in 1-inch pieces
1 cup sliced onion
1 12-ounce bottle ale
8 wieners, cut diagonally into thirds
2 tablespoons butter
¾ cup domestic red wine, such as Burgundy
1 clove garlic, finely minced

Saute the bacon in the bottom of a heavy saucepan with a tightly fitting cover until it is a delicate golden brown. Pour off the excess grease.

Rinse the sauerkraut under cold running water and then drain thoroughly and press dry. Place the rinsed sauerkraut on top of the crisped bacon. Distribute the sliced onion over the top of the sauerkraut. Add the bottle of ale and cook over moderate heat, tightly covered, for 45 minutes.

While the sauerkraut is cooking, melt the butter in a skillet and saute the wieners until they begin to brown slightly. Add the wine and the minced garlic. Turn the heat down to simmer and continue to cook over low heat until the wine has almost completely evaporated. Turn the hot dogs frequently during this cooking period.

Using a slotted spoon, remove the cooked sauerkraut and bacon pieces from their juice and mound on a platter. Place the pieces of hot dog around the outside edge. Serve piping hot. Serves 6.

HOT DOGS WITH BEANS AND CORN

8 hot dogs, cut in thirds
½ cup butter
1 cup diced celery
½ cup diced onion
½ teaspoon salt
¼ teaspoon pepper
¼ teaspoon cinnamon
⅛ teaspoon ground cumin seed (optional)
2 10-ounce cans cream of celery soup
1 10-ounce package frozen French-style green beans, thawed
1 10-ounce package frozen corn niblets, thawed

Melt the butter in a 2-quart saucepan; add the celery and onions. Saute over low heat until the celery is transparent on the edges and tender. Add the hot dogs and continue to saute until they are lightly browned. Add the salt, pepper, cinnamon and cumin. Mix well, and then add the celery soup. Continue to cook over low heat until the soup begins to bubble.

Add the green beans and the niblet corn and cook over low heat for 8 minutes longer or until the beans are tender. Turn the mixture over from time to time, taking care not to mash the vegetables. Serve piping hot. This dish is excellent with plain boiled potatoes or with broad egg noodles. Serves 6.

HOT DOG AND BEAN LOAF

2 cups dry lima beans, soaked overnight in water to cover
12 hot dogs
1 cup soft enriched bread crumbs
¼ cup peanut butter
¼ teaspoon pepper
1 teaspoon poultry seasoning
¼ cup onion, finely grated
1 tablespoon bacon or ham fat
2 eggs, slightly beaten
1 cup milk

Drain the lima beans after soaking. Cover with fresh cold water and cook over moderate heat until the beans are tender enough to pierce with a fork. Drain through a collander and allow them to cool. Chop the lima beans until they are the consistency of large peas.

Dice the hot dogs into ¼-inch cubes and add to the chopped beans. Add the bread crumbs, peanut butter, pepper, poultry seasoning, grated onion and bacon fat. Mix all very well; then gradually add the beaten egg and the milk. Mix well again. Place in a lightly greased 9x5x3-inch loaf pan. Place in a 350° F. oven for 40 minutes.

Allow the loaf to cool for 5 minutes; then loosen with a sharp knife and turn out on to a heated platter. Cut into 1½-inch slices. Serve with chili sauce or catsup.

CHINESE CABBAGE AND HOT DOGS

1 large head Chinese cabbage (about 2½ pounds)
8 hot dogs, sliced in ½-inch circles
2 teaspoons powdered mustard
¼ teaspoon salt
¼ cup soy sauce
2 teaspoons cider vinegar

Wash the Chinese cabbage under cold running water. Cut away any tough outside leaves and any tough root portion. Slice the cabbage across the grain in ¾-inch slices. Place the slices in a suitable kettle with water to cover. Bring to a rolling boil over moderate heat. Cook for 1 minute or just enough to wilt slightly. Drain thoroughly in a colander.

Place the cabbage in a large mixing bowl along with the hot dog slices. Mix the mustard, salt, soy sauce and vinegar thoroughly. Pour this mixture over the cabbage and the hot dogs. Turn several times so that the cabbage is evenly coated. Chill in the refrigerator for 2 hours before serving. Serves 6.

BRUSSEL SPROUTS AND HOT DOGS

2 10-ounce packages frozen Brussel sprouts
1 envelope dehydrated onion soup mix
2 cups hot water
8 hot dogs
1 tablespoon dehydrated parsley

Place the Brussel sprouts in a suitable saucepan. Mix the onion soup and the hot water together and pour over the Brussel sprouts. Place over moderate heat and cook for 8 minutes or until the sprouts are tender but not mushy.

Cut the hot dogs up into 1-inch lengths and add to the Brussel sprouts. Turn the heat to very low and cook for 5 minutes. Turn off the heat and allow the hot dogs and the sprouts to stand in the hot liquid for an additional 5 minutes. Do not cover.

Drain off the liquid and discard. Sprinkle the dehydrated parsley over the sprouts and hot dogs. Mix lightly and serve immediately. Serves 6.

HOT DOG ZUCCHINI COMBO

6 fairly large zucchini, about 5 inches long and 1½ inches
  in diameter
1 tablespoon salt
3 strips lean bacon, cut in ¼-inch cubes
6 hot dogs, finely chopped
½ cup onion, finely chopped
½ cup fine cracker crumbs
1 8-ounce can tomato sauce
⅛ teaspoon crushed sweet basil
½ teaspoon celery seed
1 tablespoon parsley, finely minced
⅛ teaspoon pepper
½ cup grated Cheddar cheese
½ cup grated Parmesan cheese

Wash the zucchini well, but do not peel. Place the squash
in a large kettle with water to cover. Add the salt and
cook over moderate heat, uncovered, for 15 minutes or until
tender enough to pierce with a fork. Drain and allow to
cool slightly.

Using a very sharp knife, cut the squash lengthwise; scoop
out the seedy inside portion and place in a large mixing
bowl.

Saute the bacon in a skillet until it just begins to turn
brown. Add the chopped hot dogs and continue to cook
until they begin to brown. Drain away any excess grease.
Add the bacon and the hot dogs to the squash centers.
Mix well. Add the onion, cracker crumbs and tomato sauce.
Add the sweet basil, celery seed, parsley and pepper. Mix
all thoroughly. Fill each half of the squash with the mixture and place in a lightly buttered baking dish.

Mix the Cheddar and the Parmesan cheese together and
sprinkle this over each of the stuffed squash. Place in a
325° F. oven for 25 minutes or until the cheese has become bubbly and slightly browned. Serve at once, piping
hot. Serves 6, allowing 2 halves per person.

CABBAGE ROLLS WITH HOT DOGS

1 3-to-4-pound head cabbage, with nice outside green leaves
3 cups boiling water
2 bay leaves
1 teaspoon garlic salt
¼ cup butter
1 cup chopped onion
12 hot dogs, chopped until the consistency of hamburger
⅔ cup instant rice, just as it comes from the package
½ cup dairy sour cream
½ teaspoon salt
½ teaspoon Accent
¼ teaspoon seasoned pepper
⅛ teaspoon nutmeg
1 #1 can tomato sauce (2 cups)

Remove 12 large outer leaves from the head of cabbage and wash them well. Place the leaves in a saucepan with a tightly fitting cover along with the 3 cups of boiling water. Bring to a rolling boil; then turn the heat back to simmer, cover and continue to cook for 5 minutes or until the cabbage leaves are soft and tender. Drain and set aside.

Cut the remainder of the cabbage into 4 wedges; remove the center core and discard. Using a very sharp knife, shred the remainder of the cabbage into 1/16-inch thick slices. Place this shredded cabbage over the bottom of a buttered 2-quart casserole with a tightly fitting cover. Add the bay leaves and sprinkle with the garlic salt. Set aside until you finish the stuffed rolls.

Melt the butter in a skillet and add the onion; saute until the onion begins to get transparent. Add the chopped hot dogs and saute until they just begin to get brown. Remove from the heat and add the rice, sour cream, salt, Accent, seasoned pepper and nutmeg. Mix all very well.

Place about ¼ cup of the hot dog mixture on the stem end of the softened cabbage leaf. Roll towards the outer edge, tucking in the sides as you go along. Fasten tightly with a toothpick.

Place the stuffed cabbage rolls on top of the shredded cabbage in the casserole. Pour the tomato sauce over the rolls and the shredded cabbage. Cover tightly and place in a 325° F. oven for 45 minutes. Turn the cabbage rolls over, and continue to bake for an additional 15 minutes.

Serve at once, piping hot. Serves 6, allowing two cabbage rolls per person.

SWEET AND SOUR LIMA BEANS WITH HOT DOGS

3 cups dried lima beans
1 clove garlic, finely chopped
½ teaspoon salt
¼ teaspoon pepper
½ cup onion, finely chopped
¼ cup parsley, finely chopped
⅓ cup cider vinegar
3 tablespoons granulated sugar
8 hot dogs, cut in thirds

Soak the lima beans overnight in water to cover. Then drain and cover with water again. Bring to a rolling boil and skim off any froth which may gather. Cover and continue to cook over low heat for 1 hour or until the beans are tender enough to pierce with a fork. Drain, reserving 1 cup of the liquid. Keep the beans covered so they remain warm.

Place the cup of bean liquid in a suitable saucepan; add the garlic, salt, pepper and chopped onion. Bring to a boil and continue to cook for 5 minutes. Add the parsley, vinegar, sugar and the cut-up hot dogs. Cook for an additional 3 minutes or until the hot dogs are heated through. Mix with the cooked beans and serve at once, piping hot. Serves 6.

Chapter IX

HOT DOGS IN DOUGH

BECAUSE OF the subtle spices and naturally good flavor of
hot dogs, they lend themselves well to being combined with
doughs and baking.

On today's grocery shelves there are so many convenience
doughs for breads and biscuits that the young homemaker
hardly needs knowledge beyond having a degree in carton-
opening. Convenience foods are wonderful and, for the most
part, foolproof. However, if you want some delightful thrills
and flavors, try combining your own basic ingredients for
biscuits and breads. After you have accomplished this minor
feat, try adding hot dogs!

In this chapter you will find deliciously garbed hot dogs
both in doughs which are made from scratch and from con-
venient packages.

Combining meat and bread doughs is about as old as
the art of cooking itself. One finds meat and dough combined in the recipes of those countries where meat is at a
premium both supply and price-wise. You will find that
when hot dogs are united with dough, they turn into wonderful budget stretchers and even greater flavor abettors.

HOT DOGS IN POTATO BISCUITS

3 cups hot mashed potatoes
3 eggs, separated
3 tablespoons melted butter
3 tablespoons grated Cheddar cheese
2 tablespoons parsley, finely chopped
½ teaspoon salt
¼ teaspoon pepper
3 tablespoons flour
¼ cup dairy sour cream
6 hot dogs, cut in half crosswise

Beat the egg yolks until they are lemon yellow. Add three tablespoons of the hot potato mixture to the yolks; mix well and then add the remainder of the yolks to the potatoes. Beat well; add the melted butter, cheese, parsley, salt, pepper and flour. Add the sour cream and beat the mixture for 1 minute.

Beat the egg whites until they are stiff and stand in peaks. Fold the egg whites into the potato mixture. Mound the potato mixture into 12 muffin tins which have been lightly buttered. Insert one hot-dog half, cut side down, into the center of each muffin and then mound up the muffin mixture around the hot dogs.

Place in a 350° F. oven for 20 minutes or until the surface of the muffins turn a rich golden brown. Serve at once, piping hot. Serves 6, allowing two potato biscuits per person.

HOT DOGS IN HERB BISCUITS

2 cups all-purpose flour
3 teaspoons baking powder
1 teaspoon salt
1 teaspoon poppy seed
½ teaspoon thyme
½ cup butter or margarine
¾ cup ice cold milk
6 hot dogs

Sift the flour, baking powder and salt together twice. Place in a mixing bowl along with the poppy seed and thyme. Add the butter and cut with a pastry blender until the consistency of corn meal. Stir in the ice cold milk and mix until you have a soft dough.

Place the dough on a floured board or pastry cloth and pat until about ½ inch thick. Using a floured doughnut cutter, cut into 12 doughnut-like circles.

Cut the hot dogs in half and place half a hot dog over the center of each circle. Bring up each side of the circle and pinch together, leaving the hot dog sticking out at each end. Place on a lightly buttered cooky tin and bake at 375° F. for 10 minutes or until the dough is a golden brown. Serves 6, allowing 2 per person.

HOT DOG, CHEESE AND ONION SURPRISE PIE

8 hot dogs
1 tablespoon butter
¾ cup chopped onion
1 egg, beaten until lemon yellow
½ cup water
1½ cups prepared biscuit mix
½ cup grated mild Cheddar Cheese
2 tablespoons poppy seeds
2 tablespoons melted butter (additional)

Melt the tablespoon of butter in a skillet and then add the chopped onions. Saute the onions until they are transparent and limp. Set aside to cool.

Mix the egg, water and biscuit mix until you have a soft dough, free of lumps. Add the cooled sauteed onion and the grated cheese. Mix well; divide the dough into two equal parts. Place one portion of the dough over the bottom of a buttered 8x2-inch deep round glass baking dish. Arrange the hot dogs over the dough from the center to the outer edge like the petals of a flower. Place the remaining dough on top of the hot dogs. Press it into place so that you can faintly see the outline of each hot dog. Using a sharp knife, score the dough between the hot dogs just as you would cut a pie.

Sprinkle the poppy seeds over the top of the dough and drizzle the two tablespoons of butter over the top. Place in a 400° F. oven for 25 minutes or until the top crust is a rich golden brown. Cut into portions along your previously scored markings and serve with additional chips of butter. Serves 6 to 8.

SURPRISE BISCUITS

10 hot dogs
1 teaspoon powdered mustard
¼ cup chopped sweet pickles
1 egg, slightly beaten
¼ cup chili sauce
1 tube refrigerated baking powder biscuits

Chop the hot dogs until they are the consistency of coarse corn meal. Add the mustard, sweet pickle, egg and chili sauce. Mix together thoroughly.

Flatten each half of the refrigerated baking powder biscuits until they are about 1 inch larger than they come in the can. Mound up a portion of the hot dog mixture in the middle of half the flattened biscuits. Moisten the outer edge with a little water. Press the top half of each biscuit in place over the filling; seal the outer edges well.

Place each filled biscuit in a buttered muffin tin or on a buttered cooky sheet. Bake at 400° F. for 15 minutes or until the biscuits are puffed up and a golden brown.

These hot dog filled biscuits are delightful served with a tossed green salad. Makes 12 biscuits.

HOT DOG ONION PIE

3 slices bacon, diced in ½-inch pieces
4 hot dogs, cut in ⅛-inch circles
2 cups sweet onion, such as Bermuda, cut into ½-inch cubes
3 eggs, beaten until lemon yellow
½ teaspoon salt
¼ teaspoon pepper
¾ cup half-and-half cream
1 9-inch unbaked deep pie crust
3 tablespoons grated Swiss cheese

Saute the bacon pieces until they are golden and crisp. Using a slotted spoon, remove the crisp bacon pieces from the grease and sprinkle them over the bottom of the 9-inch pie crust. Add the hot dog slices and the onion pieces to the hot bacon grease and saute until the onion is limp and transparent. Remove from the heat and set aside to cool to room temperature.

Mix the beaten eggs, cream, salt and pepper together. Stir this into the hot dog-onion mixture. Pour into the unbaked pie shell. Sprinkle the grated Swiss cheese over the top. Place in a 325° F. oven for 35 minutes or until the center is firm and a table knife comes out clean when inserted. Serve at once, piping hot. Serves 6.

HOT DOG BISCUIT PIE

1½ cups all-purpose flour
3 teaspoons baking powder
½ teaspoon salt
1 teaspoon paprika
¼ teaspoon pepper
1 teaspoon celery salt
5 tablespoons vegetable shortening
¾ cup cold milk
3 tablespoons butter
¼ cup onion, sliced ⅛ inch thick
1 10-ounce can tomato soup
8 hot dogs, finely chopped

Mix the flour, baking powder, salt, pepper, paprika and celery salt together well. Using a pastry blender or two table knives, cut in the shortening until it is the consistency of coarse corn meal. Add the cold milk and mix into a soft dough. Place on a floured board, knead lightly, and pat out until about ½ inch thick. Cut into 2-inch circles. Set aside.

Melt the butter in a skillet; add the onion and saute until it is transparent and tender. Add the tomato soup and mix well. Add the chopped hot dogs and cook until the mixture bubbles. Pour into a buttered casserole or baking dish. Place the biscuit rounds on top. Bake in a 450° F. oven for 20 minutes or until the biscuits are puffed up and a golden brown. Serve at once. Serves 6.

HOT DOG CORN BREAD PIE

8 hot dogs, cut in ¼-inch circles
½ cup onion, coarsely chopped
1 tablespoon margarine
1 8-ounce can tomato sauce
1 #2 can red kidney beans, drained
½ teaspoon salt
¼ teaspoon pepper
½ teaspoon chili powder (increase to 1 teaspoon if you like chili flavor)
½ teaspoon Accent

126

Corn Bread Topping:

1½ cups all-purpose flour
1 teaspoon salt
4 teaspoons baking powder
1 teaspoon granulated sugar
1 cup yellow corn meal
1½ cups milk
⅓ cup melted butter
3 eggs, beaten until lemon yellow

Place the hot dog pieces, onion and margarine in a large skillet; saute over low heat until the onion is transparent and the hot dogs begin to brown slightly. Add the tomato sauce, kidney beans, salt, pepper, chili powder and Accent. Mix all well and pour into a 2-quart, buttered casserole.

Sift the flour, salt, baking powder, sugar and corn meal together twice. Place in a suitable mixing bowl. Mix the milk, melted butter and the beaten eggs together, then pour into the dry ingredients. Beat with a wire whisk until smooth and free of lumps. Spoon over the top of the hot dog mixture. Bake in a 375° F. oven for 25 minutes. Serves 6.

HOT DOG CORN FRITTERS

6 eggs, separated
1 12-ounce can niblet corn with pimiento, drained
6 hot dogs, diced in ¼-inch pieces
½ cup all-purpose flour
½ teaspoon salt
1 tablespoon cooking sherry (optional but good)

Beat the egg yolks until they are light and fluffy; add the corn, the diced hot dogs, flour, salt and sherry. Mix very well.

Beat the egg whites until they stand in peaks. Fold the egg whites into the hot dog mixture, taking care not to lose the air.

Fry on a hot, lightly greased griddle as you would pancakes, using about ¼ cup of the mixture per cake. Serve at once, piping hot. Serves 6, generously.

HOT DOG PIE #1

2 cups all-purpose flour
½ teaspoon salt
⅔ cup margarine or vegetable shortening
5 brimming tablespoons ice water
1 10-ounce package frozen cauliflower, thawed to room
temperature
1 10-ounce package frozen green beans, thawed to room
temperature
6 hot dogs, diced in ½-inch cubes
½ cup onion, thinly sliced
1 10-ounce can Cheddar cheese soup

Sift the flour and salt together; add the margarine and
cut with a pastry blender until it is crumbly and about the
size of peas. Add the ice water, one tablespoon at a time,
and work into a soft dough.

Place the ball of dough on a floured board and divide
into thirds. Take ⅔ of the dough and roll out until you
have a circle which will fit the bottom and sides of a 1½-
quart casserole. Place the dough in the casserole and pinch
the edges into flutes so that the juices of the casserole will
not run out during baking.

Place the remaining ⅓ of the dough on the floured board
and roll out into a circle which will fit the top of the
casserole. Cut into six wedges just as you would cut a pie.
Place the 6 wedges on a cooky sheet. Place the lined casserole and the wedges in a 400° F. oven for 10 minutes
or until a very pale golden brown.

Cut any large pieces of cauliflower in half; place in a
large mixing bowl along with the beans, hot dog cubes,
onion and the cheese soup just as it comes from the can.
Mix all together well.

Leaving your baked pastry shell right in the casserole
in which it was baked, pour in the vegetable and hot dog
mixture. Press the ingredients down slightly so that the top
is not too mounded. Place the 6 baked wedges over the
top of the casserole. Bake in a 325° F. oven for 25 minutes
or until the cauliflower can be pierced with a fork. Serve
piping hot. Serves 4 to 6.

HOT DOG PIE #2

2 cups sifted all-purpose flour
1 teaspoon salt
⅔ cup shortening
4 brimming tablespoons ice water
1 10-ounce package frozen cauliflower, cooked according
  to package directions
1 10-ounce package frozen carrots and peas in cream
  sauce, cooked according to package directions
½ cup onion, finely chopped
1 10-ounce can Cheddar cheese soup
½ cup milk
8 hot dogs, cut in ½-inch cubes

Sift the flour and salt together twice. Place in a mixing
bowl along with the shortening. Cut with a pastry blender
until it is the consistency of corn meal. Add the water a
little at a time, and work into a soft dough. Divide the
dough in half; roll out one half to fit the bottom and sides
of a 1½-quart casserole. Roll out the remainder to fit the
top of the casserole. Set aside while you prepare the rest
of the ingredients.

Place the cauliflower and carrots and peas in a saucepan
over very low heat. Add the chopped onion, the Cheddar
cheese soup and milk. Cook until all is smoothly blended.
Stir lightly from time to time. Add the hot dogs and mix
lightly.

Pour the mixture into the waiting bottom crust in the
casserole. Cut the top crust into 6 equal wedges and lay
them on top of the hot dog and vegetable mixture. Flute
and seal the edges of the pastry where they meet on the
outer rim.

Place in a 350° F. oven for 20 minutes or until the
crust is golden brown. Serves 6.

HOT DOG DUMPLINGS

8 medium-sized potatoes
2 egg yolks, beaten until lemon yellow
1 teaspoon salt
¼ teaspoon pepper
6 strips lean bacon
6 hot dogs
½ cup chopped onion
1 tablespoon parsley, finely chopped
3 cups sifted, all-purpose flour
3 quarts water
1 tablespoon salt

Peel and quarter the potatoes. Place in a saucepan with water to cover. Cook over moderate heat for about 20 minutes or until they can be pierced with a fork. Drain and mash until light and fluffy. Allow to cool to room temperature, then add the egg yolks, salt and pepper. Whip again until the mixture is light and fluffy. Set aside.

Dice the bacon into ¼-inch pieces and place in a skillet over moderate heat. Dice the hot dogs and add to the bacon. Add the chopped onion and saute until the onion is soft and transparent. Pour off any excess grease. Remove from the heat and stir in the parsley. Set aside.

Add one half of the flour to the potato mixture; stir until mixed and smooth. Add the remaining flour and knead into a dough just as you would bread. Place on a floured board or pastry cloth and continue to knead until slightly elastic. Flatten out the dough until it is uniformly ½ inch thick. Using a 2-inch diameter biscuit cutter, cut the dough into circles. Place 1 tablespoon of the hot dog mixture on one circle and cover with another circle. Press the edges together firmly to seal and then shape into a ball.

Bring the three quarts of water to a rolling boil in a 4-quart saucepan with a tightly fitting cover. Add 1 tablespoon salt. Add the dumplings one at a time to the boiling water; cover tightly and cook for 15 minutes without removing the cover. Remove the dumplings with a slotted spoon; drain well. Place on a warm platter and serve at once. Serves 6.

Note: These dumplings may be served plain or they may be served with melted butter drizzled over them. They make a good companion to sauerkraut and also make an excellent main dish when sprinkled with ¾ cup buttered bread crumbs and placed under the broiler long enough to brown the crumbs. The dumplings can also be served in a clear soup or broth. Do not cook the dumplings in the soup, but cook them separately as directed and then add them to the hot soup at the last minute.

If you have any leftover hot dog dumplings, they are delicious if sauteed until golden brown in butter.

SWISS PIE WITH HOT DOGS

1 unbaked 10-inch pie shell
5 strips lean bacon
6 hot dogs, diced in ¼-inch cubes
1 cup shredded Swiss cheese
4 eggs, beaten until lemon yellow
2 cups half-and-half cream
½ teaspoon salt
¼ teaspoon pepper
¼ teaspoon sugar
2 drops Tabasco
⅛ teaspoon nutmeg, freshly grated

Place the unbaked crust in a 400° F. oven for 8 minutes or until it just begins to turn a pale brown. Remove from the oven and set aside. Turn oven to 450° F. to preheat while making the rest of the pie.

Place the bacon in a skillet and saute until it is crisp and brown. Remove the bacon to paper toweling to drain. Saute the hot dog cubes in the bacon drippings until they get brown around the edges; remove to paper toweling to drain. Discard the remainder of the bacon drippings.

Crumble the crisp bacon into bits and spread over the bottom of the pie crust. Sprinkle the hot dog pieces over the bacon. Sprinkle the shredded Swiss cheese over the bacon and the hot dogs.

Mix the eggs, cream, salt, pepper, sugar, Tabasco and nutmeg together well. Pour over the ingredients in the pie shell. Place in a 450° F. oven and immediately reduce the heat to 400° F. Bake at 400° F. for 10 minutes and then reduce the heat to 325° F. and bake for 30 minutes or until the center of the pie is firm and the top is a rich brown. Cut in wedges and serve. Serves 6.

PEEKING DOGS

1 cup milk
1 envelope dry, granulated yeast
¼ cup lukewarm water
¼ cup sugar
¼ cup shortening
1 teaspoon salt
4 cups sifted flour
2 eggs, beaten until lemon yellow
12 hot dogs
3 tablespoons butter
2 tablespoons poppy seed

Scald the milk in the top of a double boiler over rapidly boiling water. Remove from the heat and allow to cool. Dissolve the yeast in the ¼ cup of lukewarm water. Set aside.

Place the sugar, shortening and salt in a large mixing bowl; mix slightly and then pour the scalded milk over all. Stir until the shortening has melted. When cooled to lukewarm, add 1 cup of the sifted flour gradually. Beat until smooth. Add the softened yeast. Mix well. Gradually add half of the remaining flour and beat until smooth. Add the two well beaten eggs and mix again. Beat in enough of the remaining flour to make a soft dough. Place the dough on a well-floured board and allow it to stand in a warm place, away from drafts, for 10 minutes.

Knead the dough until it is elastic. Form the dough into a ball, and place in a greased mixing bowl. Turn the dough over so that the top is greased and shiny from being in the greased bowl. Cover, and set in a warm place for about ½ hour or until double in size. Knead again, and let rise once more until doubled in size. Knead again, and place on a lightly floured board.

Roll the dough out into a rectangle about ½ inch thick. Cut into strips ½ x ½ x 6 inches long.

Starting at one end of a hot dog, wrap the dough around the hot dog barber pole fashion. Wrap each hot dog to within ½ inch of the other end, allowing one end of the hot dog to peek out. Pinch the end piece to the rest of the dough to seal in place. Place the dough-wrapped hot dogs on a lightly buttered baking sheet. Brush with melted butter and sprinkle with poppy seed. Cover and allow the dough to rise again for 25 minutes longer.

Place in a 425° F. oven for 15 minutes or until the crust around the hot dog is a golden brown. These peeking dogs can be served either hot or cold. Makes 1 dozen.

HOT DOG PIZZA PIE

8 hot dogs, diced in ¼-inch cubes
1 cup onion, coarsely chopped, or, if you prefer, very thinly sliced
1 clove garlic, finely chopped
1 #1 can tomato sauce (2 cups)
1 teaspoon salt
¼ teaspoon seasoned pepper
1 teaspoon fennel seed
1 teaspoon oregano
1 package (1 ounce) dry yeast dissolved in ¾ cup lukewarm water
2½ cups prepared biscuit mix
½ cup all-purpose flour
1 pound Mozzarella cheese, sliced ⅛ inch thick
½ cup grated Parmesan cheese

Mix the chopped hot dogs, onion, garlic, tomato sauce, salt, pepper, fennel seed and oregano together. Place over moderate heat and bring to a rolling boil; turn the heat down and simmer for 5 minutes longer, stirring occasionally to prevent sticking. Remove from heat and set aside.

Mix the yeast dissolved in the ¾ cup lukewarm water with the prepared biscuit mix. Beat vigorously until smooth and free of lumps. Sprinkle a portion of the flour on a board or pastry cloth and knead the dough until it is smooth and glossy. Divide the dough into two parts. On a floured surface, roll each piece of dough into a 12- to 14-inch circle. Place the circle of dough on a cooky sheet and pinch and flute the edge so that the cheese and sauce cannot run out during baking.

Spread half of the hot dog and tomato mixture on each of the dough circles. Place the Mozzarella slices over the top of the sauce. Sprinkle the tops with the Parmesan cheese.

Bake in a 450° F. oven for 12 minutes or until the cheese is bubbly and the edges of the crust are a golden brown. Serve at once. Serves 6.

HOT DOG ROLL-UPS

2 cups all-purpose flour
4 teaspoons baking powder
½ teaspoon salt
4 tablespoons butter or margarine
¾ cup cold milk
8 hot dogs, very finely chopped
4 tablespoons butter (additional)
1 tablespoon prepared yellow mustard

Cheese Sauce:

2 tablespoons butter
2 tablespoons all-purpose flour
1 cup milk
1 cup grated mild Cheddar cheese

Sift the flour, baking powder and salt together twice. Using a pastry blender or two knives, cut the butter into the flour until it is the consistency of coarse corn meal. Add the milk, a little at a time, and stir until all is thoroughly mixed. Place on a floured board or pastry cloth and knead into a smooth dough.

Melt the additional butter in a saucepan over low heat, add the hot dogs and the mustard; mix well. Spread the hot dog mixture over the surface of the dough. Roll up as you would a jelly roll. Cut up into 1½-inch thick slices. Flatten each slice slightly. Place on a cooky sheet and bake in a 400° F. oven for 20 minutes or until the tops are a golden brown.

For the sauce, melt the butter in a saucepan, stir in the flour and continue to cook until it begins to bubble. Slowly add the milk and, stirring constantly, continue to cook over low heat until the mixture has thickened and coats the spoon. Add the grated cheese and continue to cook over low heat until all of the cheese has melted and the mixture is smooth and creamy.

Serve each roll-up with a topping of the cheese sauce. Serves 6, allowing one roll-up per person.

Variations:

Add ½ cup finely-chopped ripe olives to the hot dog mixture for a different flavor.

134

Add ½ cup very finely-chopped onions to the hot dog mixture.

Add ¼ cup drained pickle relish to the hot dog mixture.

Substitute ½ cup Parmesan cheese for half of the Cheddar cheese.

HOT DOGS IN A BLANKET

1 tablespoon granulated dry yeast
½ cup lukewarm water
¾ cup milk, scalded and then cooled to lukewarm
1 teaspoon salt
2 teaspoons sugar
2 cups all-purpose flour
6 hot dogs, cut in half crosswise
2 slices American cheese 3x3x⅛ inch thick

Dissolve the dry yeast in the half cup of lukewarm water. Add the salt and sugar to the cooled, scalded milk. Mix well, and then stir in the dissolved yeast. Sift the flour into the milk mixture a little at a time; mix well after each addition. Cover and set aside, away from all drafts, until doubled in bulk.

Slit each hot dog in half lengthwise; do not cut all the way through, but leave a "hinge" at the back. Cut the cheese into ½x1½-inch pieces. Place 2 pieces of cheese in each hot-dog slit.

When the dough has doubled in bulk, take a piece about as big as an egg and roll out to about the same thickness as pie dough. Shape into a wedge and place the cheese-filled hot dog at the broad end. Roll the hot dog up in the dough, folding in the sides as you go along. Place in rows in a coffee-cake tin and bake in a 375° F. oven for 35 minutes or until puffed up and golden brown. Serve either hot or cold. Makes 6.

Chapter X

GOURMET HOT DOGS

GOURMET COOKING usually brings to mind fabulous dishes like Polynesian chicken or a prime roast 7 ribs long.

When you mention hot dogs and the word gourmet in a single breath, people are inclined to look at you askance. Stare them down and hold your ground, for hot dogs can be made into some real gourmet dishes.

The flavor and spices in hot dogs lend themselves well to the festive touch and become loyal, agreeable companions to wine, brandy or fruits and vegetables often found on the gourmet's list.

HOT DOGS IN FRUITED BRANDY SAUCE

1 10-ounce can condensed bouillon
1 9-ounce can crushed pineapple
⅓ cup white raisins
2 tablespoons cornstarch
¼ cup water
½ cup grape brandy
12 hot dogs

Place the bouillon, crushed pineapple, juice and all, and white raisins in a saucepan over moderate heat. Mix the cornstarch with the water. When the bouillon begins to bubble, add the cornstarch and cook until thickened and transparent, stirring constantly. Remove from heat and stir in the brandy.

Place the hot dogs in a lightly buttered shallow baking dish. Pour the sauce over the hot dogs. Place in a 375° F. oven for 8 minutes or until heated through. Serve at once, piping hot. Serves 6, allowing 2 hot dogs per person.

FESTIVE HOT DOG SOUFFLÉ

15 hot dogs
¼ cup melted butter
1 clove garlic, sliced paper thin
¼ cup all-purpose flour
½ cup milk
1 #303 can cream-style corn
½ teaspoon salt
¼ teaspoon pepper
1 teaspoon Worcestershire sauce
2 cups grated mild Cheddar cheese
6 eggs, separated

Cut off a small portion of one end of each of the hot dogs so that they can be stood on end around the outside perimeter of a buttered 2-quart casserole. Set the hot dogs aside while you mix the soufflé.

Place the melted butter in a saucepan with the sliced garlic and cook over moderate heat until the garlic begins to brown. Using a slotted spoon, remove the pieces of garlic and discard. Add the flour to the melted butter and stir until it is smooth; slowly add the milk and, stirring constantly, continue to cook over low heat until smoothly blended and thickened. Add the corn, salt, pepper and Worcestershire sauce. Add the grated cheese and continue to cook over low heat, stirring constantly, until the cheese has melted. Remove from the heat and set aside to cool.

Beat the egg yolks until they are lemon colored. Add three tablespoons of the cheese mixture to the eggs and then add the eggs to the cheese mixture. Beat the egg whites until they stand in peaks. Gently fold the whites into the cheese mixture.

Pour the mixture into a 2-quart buttered casserole and stand each hot dog on the cut end around the outside perimeter of the casserole. Bake in a 350° F. oven for 45 minutes or until the center is firm. Serve at once, piping hot. Serves 6.

HOT DOGS IN WINE AND MUSTARD SAUCE

1 pound hot dogs
1 tablespoon cornstarch
1 tablespoon granulated sugar
1 teaspoon powdered mustard
½ teaspoon salt
½ teaspoon Accent
1 cup water
2 tablespoons butter or margarine
¼ cup cider vinegar
¼ cup Rhine wine or Sauterne
1 teaspoon grated horseradish
3 egg yolks, beaten until lemon yellow

Mix the cornstarch, sugar, mustard, salt and Accent together thoroughly. Place in the top of a double boiler along with the cup of water. Mix well, and then cook directly over the heat until slightly thickened, stirring constantly.

Now place the double boiler top over rapidly boiling water and add the butter, vinegar, Rhine wine and horseradish. Mix all thoroughly. Take 3 tablespoons of the mixture and stir into the beaten egg yolks; then add the egg yolks to the mustard mixture. Stir and mix well. Continue to cook over the boiling water until the mixture is thick and coats the spoon.

Place the hot dogs in the mustard sauce, reduce the heat under the boiling water, and cook for 15 minutes. If the hot dogs are not completely submerged in the sauce, turn them over several times during this cooking period.

Serve on warm hot dog buns with a portion of the sauce as a sandwich. These hot dogs are also delicious with potato salad. Serves 4, allowing 2 hot dogs per person.

HOT DOG OPEN FACERS

10 hot dogs, diced in ¼-inch pieces
1½ cups half-and-half cream
2 egg yolks, beaten until lemon yellow
½ teaspoon salt
¼ teaspoon pepper
2 tablespoons sherry
1 tablespoon dehydrated parsley
6 English muffins, halved and toasted

Place the cream in the top of a double boiler and heat to the scalding point. Take two tablespoons of the hot cream and stir it into the beaten egg yolks; add the beaten yolks to the cream. Cook, stirring constantly, for 3 minutes or until thickened and the mixture coats the spoon.

Add the salt, pepper, sherry and parsley. Stir well and add the diced hot dogs. Cook for an additional 3 minutes or until the hot dogs are heated through.

Place two of the English muffin halves on a serving plate and top with a generous portion of the hot-dog mixture. Serve at once, piping hot. Serves 6, allowing two muffin halves for each person.

HOT DOG SHISH KABOBS

1 pound hot dogs
2 #1 cans pineapple chunks
¼ cup soy sauce
¼ cup olive oil
¾ cup Burgundy
12 slices ranch-style bacon, approximately 10 inches long
1 #1 can pitted ripe olives, drained
24 large, pimiento-stuffed green olives
1 #2 can small boiled onions

Cut each hot dog up into 4 pieces. Place in a mixing bowl with a tightly fitting cover. Drain the pineapple chunks and reserve the juice. Place the soy sauce and olive oil in a measuring cup and then add enough of the pineapple juice to bring it up to 1 cup. Mix with the Burgundy and pour over the hot dog pieces. Cover and set aside to marinate for at least 1 hour. Turn the hot dog pieces over from time to time so that all are evenly flavored by the marinade.

Cut the bacon strips into approximate thirds and wrap a piece of bacon around each pineapple wedge. String on a skewer following with a piece of hot dog a ripe olive, a stuffed olive, a boiled onion and so on until you have used up all of the ingredients.

Brush generously with the remaining hot dog marinade. Place on a broiler rack about 4 inches from the heat or on an outside grill. Broil or grill until the bacon is crisp and golden. Baste with the marinade frequently during this time. Serve piping hot. Serves 6 generously.

HOT DOG RICH BOY SANDWICHES

8 hot dogs
8 slices Swiss cheese, ⅛ inch thick
8 slices boiled ham, 1/16 inch thick
4 miniature loaves French Bread (baked, not the bake-and-serve variety)
¼ cup melted butter
1 10-ounce package frozen broccoli spears, thawed
1 10-ounce package frozen French fried onion rings, thawed
1 cup dairy sour cream
2 egg yolks, beaten until lemon yellow
½ teaspoon salt
1 tablespoon lemon juice
⅛ teaspoon powdered mustard
1 drop Tabasco

Using a very sharp knife, make criss-cross gashes about ⅛ inch deep along the side of each hot dog. Place a slice of Swiss cheese on top of a slice of boiled ham; place the hot dog at one end of the cheese and ham and roll it up. Fasten the cheese and ham in place with a toothpick. Leave the toothpick protruding so that it can be removed before serving.

Cut the French bread loaves in half lengthwise and scoop out the soft interior, leaving a wall about ½ inch thick. Brush the insides of the bread shells with the melted butter. Place several broccoli spears at each end of the bread shell with the blossom portion facing toward the outside. Place one of the ham-cheese wrapped hot dogs on top of the broccoli stems in the center of the loaf half. Place the loaf halves on a lightly buttered cooky tin. Arrange a portion of the French fried onion rings along the sides and over the top of each hot dog. Place in a 325° F. oven for 25 minutes or until the white portion of the bread turns a golden brown.

Meanwhile, whip the sour cream until it is light and fluffy. Add the beaten eggs, salt, lemon juice, mustard and Tabasco. Whip again for a second or two so that all of the ingredients are well mixed. Place the mixture in the top of a double boiler over water which is kept just below the boiling point. Do not let the water boil, for this will curdle the sauce. Stirring constantly, cook the mixture over the warm water until it thickens and coats the spoon. Avoid overcooking, as this will cause the sauce to get lumpy. The moment it coats the spoon, remove from the heat. The sauce can be left uncovered over the hot water until you are ready to use it. Stir from time to time to prevent the surface from getting dry.

Place the baked French bread sandwiches on individual serving plates. Remove the toothpicks from the ham-cheese wrapping. Spoon a generous amount of the sauce over each sandwich. Serve at once, piping hot. Serves 8.

DRUNKEN DOGS

1 cup sour-mash bourbon
1 cup catsup
1 cup dark brown sugar
¼ cup onion, very finely chopped
1 pound hot dogs or 1 pound small Vienna-style wieners

Note: Sour-mash bourbon is an absolute "must" for this recipe; if you use an ordinary bourbon, you will not gain the same delicious flavor.

Place the sour-mash bourbon, catsup and brown sugar in a large skillet with a tightly fitting cover. Place over very low heat and cook, stirring constantly, until the sugar has melted. Add the onion and mix well.

If you are using the regular-sized hot dogs, cut them up into five pieces. Distribute the hot dogs in the sauce. Spoon some of the sauce over the hot dogs so that they are well coated. Cover and continue to cook over very low heat for 45 minutes. Keep heat just below the simmering point. Stir gently and spoon the sauce over the hot dogs frequently during this cooking time. If the liquid does diminish somewhat, add a little extra bourbon.

Serve on a hot platter or in a candle-heated serving dish with the sauce surrounding the hot dogs. Place a colorful cocktail pick in each piece of hot dog. If you wish, serve rounds of soft white bread on a separate plate for your guests. Serves 12.

HOT DOGS WITH A FRENCH TOUCH

2 10-ounce packages frozen French-style green beans, cooked according to package directions; do not drain after cooking
10 hot dogs, sliced in ½-inch circles
1 cup mayonnaise
3 hard-boiled eggs, peeled and chopped
2 tablespoons lemon juice
2 tablespoons minced onion
1 teaspoon Worcestershire sauce
½ teaspoon powdered mustard
½ teaspoon garlic salt
2 drops Tabasco

Drop the hot-dog circles into the undrained, hot cooked French-style green beans; place over very low heat for 5 minutes.

Place the mayonnaise in the top of a double boiler over slowly boiling water. Add the hard-boiled eggs, lemon juice, onion, Worcestershire sauce, powdered mustard, garlic salt and Tabasco. Mix well and cook over the slowly boiling water for 8 minutes.

Drain the hot dogs and beans thoroughly. Place on a heated platter and pour the hot sauce over them. Serve at once. Serves 6.

GOURMET HOT DOG VEAL LOAF

12 hot dogs
1 pound double-ground veal
¼ pound lean salt pork, double ground with the veal
2 eggs
2 cups soft, enriched white bread crumbs
1 teaspoon salt
¼ teaspoon pepper
2 tablespoons grated onion
¼ cup lemon juice
½ teaspoon paprika
2 10-inch slices lean bacon

Chop the hot dogs until they are the consistency of coarse corn meal. Add the chopped hot dogs to the ground veal and ground salt pork. Mix and knead until all is well blended. Set aside.

In a mixing bowl, beat the eggs until they are lemon yellow; add the bread crumbs, salt, pepper, grated onion and the lemon juice. Mix all very well. Add the veal-hot dog mixture and again mix and knead until all is thoroughly blended.

Form into an oblong loaf and place in a lightly buttered oblong baking dish. Sprinkle the top of the loaf with the paprika. Cut the bacon slices in half and place the four pieces of bacon diagonally over the top of the loaf. Bake in a 400° F. oven for 30 minutes. Then reduce the heat to 300° F. and bake for 1½ hours. Remove from the oven and allow to cool for 5 minutes before slicing. Slice in generous 1½-inch slices. Serves 6.

Note: This loaf is also delicious served cold and makes excellent sandwiches.

HOT DOGS SUPREME WITH BEANS

8 hot dogs, diced in ½-inch cubes
2 tablespoons brandy
½ cup French dressing
2 10-ounce packages frozen whole green beans, cooked according to package directions and then chilled
¼ cup red Italian onion, thinly sliced and separated into rings
1 cup celery, sliced 1/16 inch thick
6 lettuce cups

Place the hot dogs in a bowl with a tightly fitting cover. Mix the brandy and French dressing and pour over the hot dogs. Toss lightly so that all is evenly coated. Cover and place in the refrigerator for 1 hour.

Mix the chilled, cooked green beans, onion rings and celery. Add the chilled hot dogs and their dressing. Toss all lightly. Serve portions in the lettuce cups. Serves 6.

Variations:

Use 2 #2 cans green beans, drained, in place of the frozen beans.
Substitute a bed of snipped water cress for the lettuce cups.

EGGPLANT AND HOT DOG MOUNDS

1 large 4-inch diameter eggplant
1 teaspoon Accent
1 teaspoon salt
6 slices lean bacon, diced in ¼-inch cubes
6 hot dogs, finely chopped
1 tablespoon onion, finely minced
½ cup butter
2 tablespoons dehydrated parsley

Wash and peel the eggplant. Slice into ¾-inch slices. Mix the Accent and salt together and sprinkle a portion on each side of the slices. Set aside and allow the excess water to drain from the eggplant.

Place the bacon in a large skillet and saute until it is a golden brown. Add the chopped hot dogs and onion. Saute until the hot dogs are slightly browned. Remove from the grease with a slotted spoon and set aside. Add several spoonfuls of the butter to the bacon grease and permit it to melt over low heat.

Meanwhile, drain the eggplant and pat each slice dry with paper toweling. Place the slices in the melted butter and saute over low heat until each slice is golden brown and tender. Add more butter as you need it for browning. Place the browned slices of eggplant in an oven-proof baking dish.

Mound a portion of the hot dog and bacon mixture in the center of each slice of eggplant. Sprinkle with a bit of parsley. Place in a 350° F. oven for 10 minutes. Serve piping hot. Serves 6 generously.

HOT DOGS AND BAKED EGGS WITH SHERRY SAUCE

½ cup melted butter
¾ cup canned mushrooms, sliced ⅛ inch thick
6 eggs
½ teaspoon salt
¼ teaspoon pepper
6 hot dogs
1 12-ounce bottle ale
½ teaspoon marjoram
½ teaspoon savory
¼ cup cooking sherry
¾ cup chili sauce
a sprinkle of cayenne
2 tablespoons minced parsley

Place 1 tablespoon of the melted butter in the bottom of each of 6 custard cups. Swirl the butter around so that it coats the sides of the cups. Divide the mushrooms into 6 portions and place in the bottom of each custard cup. Carefully break each egg into the custard cup on top of the mushrooms. Sprinkle each egg with a bit of the salt and pepper. Place the custard cups in a shallow pan of water in a 350° F. oven for 15 minutes or until the yolk is coated over and the egg is fairly firm.

Meanwhile, mix the ale, marjoram and savory. Place over moderate heat and bring to a boil. Add the hot dogs, and allow them to stand in the hot beer for 10 minutes.

Mix the sherry, chili sauce and cayenne together and place over moderate heat until the mixture begins to bubble. Turn the heat back to simmer and cook for 5 minutes, stirring occasionally.

Remove the hot dogs from the ale and slice each hot dog into ⅛-inch slices. Place one sliced hot dog on top of the firm baked eggs. Top each hot dog with two tablespoons of the sauce and a sprinkle of parsley. Serve piping hot. Serves 6.

HOT DOGS IN SOUR CREAM SAUCE

12 hot dogs
¼ cup butter
¼ cup flour
½ cup catsup
½ teaspoon salt
¼ teaspoon pepper
2 tablespoons parsley, finely chopped
1 cup dairy sour cream

Cut the hot dogs up into thirds crosswise. Set aside. Melt the butter in a 1-quart saucepan. Stir in the flour and cook over low heat until smooth and bubbly. Add the catsup and mix again until smooth. Add the cut-up hot-dog pieces, salt, pepper and parsley. Mix well. Cook over very low heat for 8 minutes or until the hot dogs are heated through.

Add the dairy sour cream and stir lightly until thoroughly mixed. Place over very low heat for 2 minutes or until the cream is heated through. Do not overcook or bring to a boil, for the sour cream will curdle. Serve piping hot. Serves 6.

Chapter XI

HOT DOGS AND THE OUTDOOR
GRILL

COOKING over an outdoor grill has become as much a way of food preparation as cooking on a conventional stove. Summer brings spirals of flavor-laden smoke from almost every back yard or patio. There are as many styles of grills as there are models of automobiles. Whether you boast a resplendent chrome and enamel rig on wheels or just an old bucket with holes punched in it and a piece of screening, you can turn out delicious food with that all-important charcoal flavor.

Hot dogs and grilling have always been highly compatible. The two have been going together since the days of the "wiener roast," when each person roasted his own hot dog on a long sharp stick over a circle of stones filled with a glowing fire.

This chapter not only contains recipes for the outdoor grill, but some that can be prepared right in your own oven when outdoor cooking is impossible.

DILLY DOGS

8 hot dogs
18 2-inch diameter salad potatoes
½ cup melted butter
½ cup fresh dill, very finely chopped

Boil the potatoes in their jackets until they are just barely tender. Chill under cold running water and then peel.

Cut the hot dogs into thirds. Brush the hot dogs and the potatoes on all sides with the melted butter. Using four pieces of hot dogs and three potatoes per skewer, string them alternately; start and end with a piece of hot dog. Sprinkle them on all sides with the finely-chopped dill.

Place over the grill about 6 inches from the coals for about 5 minutes. Turn to grill evenly. Serve at once, piping hot. Serves 6.

147

OREGANO HOT DOG GRILL

12 hot dogs
2 cloves garlic, finely minced
½ teaspoon salt
¾ cup olive oil
½ cup dry red wine
¼ teaspoon pepper
1 tablespoon oregano, finely crushed

Partially split the hot dogs in half lengthwise. Do not cut all the way through, but leave a "hinge" at the back.

Mix the garlic, salt, olive oil, wine, pepper and oregano together. Pour into the bottom of a shallow pan large enough to accomodate the hot dogs laying flat with the open side down.

Place the hot dogs, cut side down in the marinade and place in the refrigerator for 3 hours or overnight if possible.

Place the hot dogs on a grill about 6 inches away from heat with the opening closed. If necessary, fasten the hot dogs back together with a toothpick. Baste with the remainder of the marinade during the cooking. Serve at once, piping hot. Serves 6, allowing 2 hot dogs per person.

SAUCEPAN GRILL

This recipe is included under grilled hot dogs because it is an excellent way to prepare them when the charcoal just won't start or when the grill is crowded with other good things to eat.

12 hot dogs
1 cup chopped onion
3 tablespoons butter
1 cup chopped celery (include some leaves)
2 8-ounce cans tomato sauce
⅛ teaspoon pulverized sweet basil
½ teaspoon salt
½ teaspoon Accent
¼ teaspoon pepper
½ cup warm water

Place the onion and the butter in a saucepan which is large enough to hold the hot dogs without too much crowding. Cook the onions over moderate heat until they are limp and transparent. Add the celery and tomato sauce and mix well. Continue to cook over moderate heat; add the sweet basil, salt, Accent, pepper and water. Mix well and bring to a bubbling boil.

Place the hot dogs in the bubbling sauce and turn the heat back to simmer. Simmer the hot dogs, turning occasionally, for 30 minutes.

Serve on buns with a little of the sauce spread on the inside of each bun. Serves 6, allowing 2 per person.

DOGS GRILLED SUPREMELY

12 hot dogs
12 slices enriched white bread, lightly buttered
1 8-ounce can tomato sauce
2 cups grated mild Cheddar cheese
2 tablespoons grated onion
½ cup peanut oil
½ cup pimiento-stuffed olives, finely chopped
¼ teaspoon salt
¼ teaspoon pepper
1 drop Tabasco

Slice the hot dogs in half lengthwise, and then cut them in half crosswise. Arrange the four pieces of hot dog on each piece of buttered bread.

Place the tomato sauce in a bowl along with the cheese, onion, oil, olives, salt, pepper and Tabasco. Mix all very well. Put a large spoonful of the mixture over the slices of hot dog. Flatten the mixture so that it covers the hot dogs but does not go over the sides of the bread. Place the slices of bread on a cooky sheet about 6 inches away from the broiler heat. Broil until the topping is melted and bubbly. Serve at once; serves 6, allowing two sandwiches per person.

HOT DOG BARBECUE

12 hot dogs
1 cup catsup
1 cup water
¼ cup brown sugar, tightly packed
¼ cup cider vinegar
¼ cup Worcestershire sauce
1 tablespoon celery seed
1 teaspoon chili powder
½ teaspoon salt
⅛ teaspoon pepper
2 drops Tabasco
12 hot dog buns
½ cup melted butter
½ teaspoon garlic powder

Gash each hot dog diagonally in four places. Set aside. Mix the catsup, water, brown sugar, cider vinegar and Worcestershire sauce in a saucepan and place over moderate heat until it reaches a rapid boil. Add the celery seed, chili powder, salt, pepper and Tabasco. Mix well and continue to cook over low heat for 15 minutes.

Brush each hot dog with the sauce and place on a grill about 6 to 8 inches away from the hot coals. Turn and brush the hot dogs with the sauce until they are a rich brown.

Mix the butter and the garlic powder together. Brush the inside of the hot dog buns with the mixture and lightly toast them over the grill. Place the barbecued hot dog in the garlic flavored bun. Add a drizzle of the basting sauce and serve. Serves 6, allowing 2 hot dogs per person.

HOT DOG AND KRAUT GRILL

1 cup sauerkraut, drained and rinsed
½ cup tart apple, peeled, cored and sliced
¼ teaspoon caraway seed
1 teaspoon brown sugar
12 hot dogs
12 strips bacon
12 hot dog buns

Place the rinsed sauerkraut and the apple pieces in a chopping bowl. Add the caraway seed; chop until the consistency of coarse corn meal. Place in a saucepan over moderate heat and add the brown sugar. Stirring frequently, cook for 8 minutes.

Split each hot dog just halfway through lengthwise, leaving a "hinge" at the back. Fill the opening with a portion of the sauerkraut mixture. Starting at one end, wrap the bacon barber pole fashion, around the hot dog. Fasten the bacon in place with toothpicks.

Place the filled and wrapped hot dogs on the grill about 6-inches away from the heat. Grill, turning from time to time, until the bacon is crisp and golden. Place each in a warm hot dog bun and serve. Serves 6, allowing 2 per person.

HOT DOG BARBECUE IN THE OVEN

12 hot dogs, cut in half lengthwise
4 tablespoons bacon or ham fat
½ cup onion, diced in ¼-inch cubes
2 cloves garlic, finely chopped
½ cup warm water
¼ cup fresh lemon juice
1 teaspoon paprika
1 teaspoon prepared mustard
¼ teaspoon seasoned pepper
½ teaspoon salt
½ teaspoon Accent
½ teaspoon grated horseradish
1 tablespoon Worcestershire sauce
¾ cup catsup

Arrange the halves of the hot dogs, cut side down, over the bottom of a shallow baking dish.

Place the bacon fat in a saucepan over moderate heat; add the diced onion and saute until the onion is limp and transparent. Add the garlic and saute for a few minutes longer. Add the warm water, lemon juice, paprika and mustard. Bring to a boil and cook for 1 minute. Remove from the heat and then add the salt, pepper, Accent, horseradish and Worcestershire sauce. Stir in the catsup. Mix all very well and then pour over the hot dogs.

Cover the pan with aluminum foil and place in a 325° F. oven for 20 minutes. Serve piping hot. Serves 6.

HOT DOG AND SPICED CRAB APPLE GRILL

8 hot dogs
1 16-ounce jar spiced crab apples (you'll need at least 12 apples)
2 tablespoons fresh lemon juice
¼ cup honey
1 teaspoon prepared mustard
1 teaspoon grated lemon rind
1 tablespoon brandy

Cut the hot dogs into thirds. Drain the juice from the crab apples and save. Cut each crab apple in half lengthwise through the core. Alternately place six pieces of hot dog and six apple halves on a skewer.

Place on a grill about 8 inches away from the heat. Grill for 10 minutes.

Mix the crab apple juice, lemon juice, honey, mustard, lemon rind and brandy together. Brush each skewer generously with the mixture and return to the grill until the glaze begins to turn brown on the hot dogs. Serve at once. Serves 6.

HOT DOGS IN BARBECUE SAUCE #1

(A delicious way to oven-grill hot dogs)

8 hot dogs
2 tablespoons peanut oil
1 cup onion, coarsely chopped
1 clove garlic, finely chopped
¼ cup green pepper, finely chopped
2 tablespoons minced parsley
¼ cup lemon juice
½ cup water
1 teaspoon paprika
1 teaspoon prepared yellow mustard
¼ teaspoon seasoned pepper
2 tablespoons brown sugar
1 tablespoon Worcestershire sauce
1 teaspoon horseradish
½ cup chili sauce

Halve the hot dogs lengthwise. Arrange them in two rows

over the bottom of a suitable buttered baking dish, cut side down.

Place the peanut oil in a large skillet; add the onion and saute until the onion is slightly brown. Add the garlic, green pepper and parsley. Continue to cook over low heat. Combine the lemon juice, water and paprika and add to the sauteed onions.

Mix the mustard, pepper, brown sugar, Worcestershire sauce, horseradish and chili sauce well. Add to the ingredients in the skillet and simmer for 8 minutes longer. Stir frequently to prevent sticking. Pour this mixture over the hot dogs.

Cover the baking dish with aluminum foil and place in a 325° F. oven for 25 minutes. Serve piping hot. Serves 6.

HOT DOGS IN BARBECUE SAUCE #2

¾ cup onion, coarsely chopped
¾ cup green pepper, coarsely chopped
2 cups tomato juice
1 cup cider vinegar
½ cup catsup
3 tablespoons Worcestershire sauce
1 stick butter
½ teaspoon salt
½ teaspoon sugar
12 hot dogs

In a 1½-quart saucepan, place the onion, green pepper and tomato juice. Bring to a rolling boil and add the vinegar, catsup, Worcestershire sauce and butter. Continue to cook over moderate heat until the butter has melted. Add the salt and sugar. Mix well. Turn the heat to simmer, cover and continue to cook at simmer for 30 minutes or until thickened.

Place the hot dogs in the sauce and cook for 8 to 10 minutes or until heated through. Serve each hot dog with a portion of the sauce over and around it. Serves 6, allowing two per person. This sauce is also excellent when serving hot dogs on buns.

GRILLED FRANKS ON A SKEWER

8 hot dogs
18 small boiled or canned potatoes
18 small canned onions
¾ cup chili sauce
2 drops Tabasco
2 tablespoons Worcestershire sauce
½ teaspoon garlic salt
¼ teaspoon black pepper

Cut the hot dogs into thirds (this will give you 24 pieces). Mix the chili sauce, Tabasco, Worcestershire sauce, garlic salt and black pepper together. Place the hot dog pieces in this mixture and allow them to marinate for at least 2 hours. Turn the pieces over so that the flavors are evenly distributed during the marinating time.

Alternate four pieces of the marinated hot dog with one each of a potato and onion on skewers, ending up with a piece of hot dog on the end. This will fill 6 skewers.

Place the skewers on the grill about 6 inches away from the heat. Brush the hot dogs, potatoes and onions from time to time with the remaining marinade. Grill until the potatoes just begin to brown. Serve at once, piping hot. Serves 6.

INDEX